T0108996

Stretching and Exploiting Thresholds for High-Order War

How Russia, China, and Iran Are Eroding American Influence Using Time-Tested Measures Short of War

Ben Connable, Jason H. Campbell, Dan Madden

Prepared for the United States Army

For more information on this publication, visit www.rand.org/t/rr1003

Library of Congress Cataloging-in-Publication Data is available for this publication.

ISBN 978-0-8330-9044-7

www.rand.org

Preface

This report describes how the United States has struggled to counter competing nation-states' use of measures short of war and how these competitors are exploiting and stretching U.S. strategic thresholds in Europe, Asia, and the Middle East. We conducted the research for this report for the U.S. Army.

The purpose of this report is to highlight this dangerous strategic trend to U.S. policymakers and military service chiefs with the intent of generating further discussion. Future RAND research will expound upon the findings and considerations in this report.

This research was sponsored by the U.S. Army and conducted within the RAND Arroyo Center's Strategy, Doctrine, and Resources Program. RAND Arroyo Center, part of the RAND Corporation, is a federally funded research and development center sponsored by the United States Army.

The Project Unique Identification Code (PUIC) for the project that produced this document is HQD146848.

For more information on RAND Arroyo Center, contact the director of operations (telephone 310-393-0411, extension 6419, fax 310-451-6952; email Marcy_Agmon@rand.org), or visit Arroyo's website at http://www.rand.org/ard.html.

Contents

Figure

Summary

This report describes how Russia, China, and Iran have used measures short of war to exploit and stretch U.S. strategic thresholds for high-order conventional or nuclear conflict in eastern Europe, east Asia, and the Middle East. Measures short of war include every action and tool at a nation-state's disposal that might further the state's interests *without* crossing the threshold into high-order and often-unmanageable interstate war. These range from simple negotiation to assassination to the use of military special operations forces. If applied in the right combinations, measures short of war can be used to achieve strategic objectives or to create room for further maneuvers against other, competing nation-states. Cunning and aggressive application of these measures can allow a nation-state—including the United States—to reshape, or stretch, the negotiated, stated, or tacit thresholds for aggressive national behavior.

Although we completed this report in early 2015, it remained under U.S. Department of Defense security review from April 2015 through its publication in April 2016. Despite the delay, the findings of this report remain unchanged. Indeed, recent posturing by both Russia and China suggests that threshold stretching and exploitation are, if anything, exacerbated. Similarly, this report is consistent with the voluminous material on "gray-zone" warfare published throughout 2015 and early 2016.

We use the following definitions for the purposes of this report:

- *high-order war:* a state-on-state conflict that includes one or more of the following: a declaration of interstate war; large-scale protracted or strategically decisive conventional combat; or a nuclear attack or nuclear exchange
- *threshold:* a negotiated, declared, or tacitly understood delimiter between measures short of war and high-order conflict (such as full-scale conventional or nuclear war)
- *threshold stretching:* applying measures short of war to force movement or change in the nature of a threshold to gain greater regional influence, access, and control
- *threshold exploitation:* taking advantage of a competitor's inability to enforce or miscalculation of a declared or tacit threshold for high-order war.

A negotiated or stated threshold has formal basis in a document, such as a treaty. For example, during the Cold War, both the North Atlantic Treaty Organization (NATO) Washington treaty of 1949 and the Warsaw Security Pact of 1955 established negotiated and stated thresholds for the use of military force by both sides.[1] A tacit threshold is more complex: It exists only through independently agreed-upon, undeclared, yet mutual understanding. Some-

---

[1] North Atlantic Treaty, April 4, 1949; Treaty of Friendship, Cooperation and Mutual Assistance Between the People's Republic of Albania, the People's Republic of Bulgaria, the Hungarian People's Republic, the German Democratic Repub-

times, these tacit thresholds are clear, stable, and effective; in other cases, they are murky, shifting, and misperceived by one side or both. The nuclear-armed states of Pakistan and India have not recently invaded or destroyed each other with nuclear weapons in great part because of an existing tacit, mutually beneficial threshold for high-order war. Israeli leaders, on the other hand, misunderstood the tacit threshold for high-order war they believed they had established with Egypt during the late 1960s and early 1970s low-intensity War of Attrition. They were then taken by surprise when Egypt escalated to high-order war and invaded Israel in 1973.

Instead of crossing negotiated, stated, and tacit thresholds, NATO, the Warsaw Pact countries, Pakistan, and India instead engaged (and engage in) aggressive use of measures short of war to achieve their national objectives. Warsaw Pact forces did not cross the Fulda Gap in central Germany to conduct an invasion of western Europe during the Cold War, but both sides used a broad range of measures short of war to compete with each other both in Europe and around the world. Pakistan and India have avoided war in the Kashmir region but have engaged in an extended tit-for-tat series of exchanges using measures short of war, including limited artillery exchanges and the alleged use of proxy terror attacks. All nations have and continue to use a broad range of diplomatic, economic, covert, informational, and limited military actions to achieve their objectives or gain advantage over local and global competitors.

Since 9/11, U.S. interests overseas appear to be increasingly vulnerable to measures short of war. It also appears that the United States is struggling to address competitors' efforts to stretch and exploit both negotiated and tacit thresholds. In the past decade, Russia used covert action, limited military incursions, and propaganda to effectively seize parts of Ukraine; China has used diplomacy, economic pressure, and limited yet aggressive military demonstrations to expand its influence in the East and South China Seas; and Iran used covert action, economic investment, and religious pressure to further its interests in Iraq at great U.S. expense. At least through mid-2015, the U.S. responses to these actions have been halting and—arguably—for the most part, ineffective. This is due in part to the predilection of some U.S. strategists to rely on outmoded and ineffective linear models of war thresholds or to assume that there are some commonly accepted and enduring interstate boundaries for engagement in high-order conflict. The gray areas of tacit regional thresholds have proven particularly difficult to assess in the three cases addressed in this report. Because neither war nor actions short of war play out on a linear scale or hew to fixed thresholds, these assumptions have contributed to U.S. vulnerability to measures short of war.

There have been many recent attempts to describe the practical complexities of measures short of war. Some argue that the use of measures short of war constitutes a new international order, or perhaps a revolution in warfare. General Sir Rupert Anthony Smith (British Army, retired) argues that interstate conflict is now a constant condition and that all wars are now wars among the people.[2] Both of these paradigms are accurate, but they are not new. Other experts on conflict have furthered the term *unrestricted warfare* to describe the use of measures short of war. Some of the ways in which measures short of war are used, and some advanced technical measures, are indeed new. However, *unrestricted warfare* is simply a catchphrase for long-standing practice. Use of measures short of war is neither unrestricted nor warfare.

---

lic, the Polish People's Republic, the Rumanian People's Republic, the Union of Soviet Socialist Republics, and the Czechoslovak Republic, May 14, 1955.

[2] Rupert Smith, *The Utility of Force: The Art of War in the Modern World*, New York: Knopf, 2007.

If the United States is to preclude further erosion of its global influence by nation-state competitors, it will have to address the problems of threshold exploitation and stretching. Policymakers and the military services should consider ways to better identify, forestall, and counteract the use of measures short of war against U.S. and allied interests. Effective counter-measures will help defend against exploitation of the inevitable weak spots in U.S. strategic capabilities. Developing more-adroit ways of countering measures short of war will help the services to develop their own measures to better exploit similar weaknesses in nation-state competitors. The first step in generating these improvements is to recognize that neither linear threshold paradigms nor revolutionary terms are sufficient to explain such events as Crimea or Iraq. U.S. strategy and capabilities must be matched to the long-standing realities of complex, multifaceted interstate competition.

Acknowledgments

We would like to thank all of the experts who contributed insight to our research, including RAND analysts Andrew Scobell, Peter A. Wilson, Olga Oliker, and Peter Chalk.

Abbreviations

ADIZ	air defense identification zone
CIA	Central Intelligence Agency
DoD	U.S. Department of Defense
NATO	North Atlantic Treaty Organization
NSC	National Security Council
NSC-68	National Security Council Paper 68
PLA	People's Liberation Army
SDF	Self-Defense Forces

CHAPTER ONE

Time-Tested Measures Short of War

This report describes a dangerous strategic weakness of the United States and explains how global competitors have taken advantage of this weakness in ways that have eroded U.S. influence. In doing so, it questions those who propose that America's competitors have latched on to a new paradigm of international behavior in order to seek advantage. It proposes instead that, although the United States is making excellent use of economic leverage, it has generally failed to maintain its competitive edge in what has been a long-standing, continuous struggle for international influence. Chapter Four poses questions relevant for the U.S. military's role in addressing this strategic weakness. It also identifies risks associated with both insufficient *and* overly aggressive improvements. Issues and lessons in this report are relevant for all elements of the U.S. government, but the considerations are designed to inform more-specific recommendations for military capabilities.

In the past ten years, three countries that compete with the United States and its allies for global and regional influence—Russia, China, and Iran—have pursued strategies that have allowed them to broaden their geographic control, to undercut U.S. allies, and to effectively erode U.S. influence in east Asia, Europe, and the Middle East.[1] Although Al Qaida and other groups misjudged U.S. thresholds for the overt and decisive use of force in the early 2000s, Russia, China, and Iran have leveraged what former U.S. diplomat and scholar George F. Kennan called "measures short of war" to aggressively further their interests while intentionally or unintentionally reducing U.S. influence and prestige: Russia successfully annexed the Crimean Peninsula; China has expanded its national airspace beyond internationally recognized boundaries and moved closer to annexing various island chains in the East China Sea; and Iran undercut the U.S. military and its allies in Iraq. In each case, the United States and its allies made it clear that they had strategic interests at stake, yet they have responded haltingly, cautiously, and, for the most part, unsuccessfully. These setbacks—and the methods used to achieve them—represent a continuing threat to U.S. strategic interests and power.

Measures short of war is a term traditionally used to describe all national ways and means available to help policymakers achieve geopolitical objectives *without* crossing the line into major conventional or (since 1945) nuclear confrontation. Kennan lists a range of these, from negotiation to embargo to intimidation, covert subversion, assassination, and the limited use of military force.[2] Measures short of war were the primary levers of geopolitical influence during

---

[1] We selected these cases based on an informed subjective analysis of available cases, the local and global impact of each case, and the centrality of these three countries to U.S. foreign policy.

[2] George F. Kennan, in Giles D. Harlow and George C. Maerz, eds., *Measures Short of War: The George F. Kennan Lectures at the National War College, 1946–1947*, Washington, D.C.: National Defense University Press, 1991, pp. 4–14.

the Cold War (1945–1991). For example, in the late 1940s, the United States contributed money to anticommunist politicians and distributed anticommunist propaganda to influence the Italian national election.[3] In the 1970s and 1980s, the United States provided indirect and mostly covert support to guerrillas fighting against the Soviet Union in Afghanistan.[4] And from the early 1960s through the end of the Vietnam War, the Soviet Union contributed military advisers and hardware to North Vietnam in an effort to undermine U.S. strategy in Southeast Asia.[5] Although new terms, such as *hybrid warfare*, are now used to describe Cold War–like activities, these specific examples are representative of standard—and long-standing—practices in international behavior.[6] The bilateral, nuclear-era Cold War theories of military escalation that still dominate U.S. strategic thinking embody a false and dangerously misleading paradigm of set-piece escalation and fixed thresholds.

This report describes and rejects claims that Russian, Chinese, and Iranian actions (among others) represent a new paradigm of international conflict. It argues that the success of these nation-states derives more simply from the aggressive mixing of old tactics and new technologies; the paradigm is old, but the effectiveness of U.S. rivals is increased for a variety of complex and often contextual reasons. Russia, China, and Iran have successfully identified, exploited, and, in some cases, stretched U.S. thresholds for high-order warfare, sometimes by careful design and sometimes by reckless, less-thoughtful, yet successful application of measures short of war. The United States is particularly vulnerable to measures short of war for two reasons: (1) U.S. strategic thought is rooted in an old, yet unrealistic, paradigm of realist, linear escalation; and (2) U.S. global reach reduces U.S. policymakers' ability to continually and successfully assess and defend tacit thresholds. Rival states have succeeded in areas that are strategically important yet peripheral to traditional U.S. interests (e.g., Crimea), but they have also exploited and stretched thresholds for war in such places as Iraq and the East China Sea. Addressing these problems and curtailing further losses require U.S. policymakers to reconsider the inadequate theories of the past without chasing new theories that are equally inadequate or inappropriate to the problem at hand.

Myths of the New Paradigms

Some argue that the failure of U.S. policy to stem these actions signals the emergence of two new paradigms of international force: (1) Force is a constant, and conflicts of all kinds are now inextricably linked to civilian populations; and (2) there are no longer any rules to international conflict. Both of these assumptions are at least partly accurate, but neither is new. Instead, some combinatory parts of these two theories—constant war among the people and unrestricted war—are probably more accurate as a paradigm for international conflict and war.

---

[3] James E. Miller, "Taking Off the Gloves: The United States and the Italian Elections of 1948," *Diplomatic History*, Vol. 7, No. 1, January 1983, pp. 35–56.

[4] See H. Sidky, "War, Changing Patterns of Warfare, State Collapse, and Transnational Violence in Afghanistan: 1978–2001," *Modern Asian Studies*, Vol. 41, No. 4, July 2007, pp. 849–888.

[5] For example, see "Declassified Government Reports to Document USSR Personnel in VN," archive summary, Texas Tech University Vietnam Online Archives, undated. Examples of this kind of Cold War behavior are ubiquitous. For example, also see Willy Brandt, "The Means Short of War," *Foreign Affairs*, January 1961.

[6] See Frank G. Hoffman, "Hybrid Warfare and Challenges," *Joint Forces Quarterly*, No. 52, first quarter 2009.

For the first part, Rupert Smith and Robert Haddick claim that the use of force and high-order war have changed because now they must be conducted among the people rather than in a vacuum of conventional military activity. In response to the question, "Is there a change in the paradigm of war?" Smith responded,[7]

> Yes, I believe that in recent decades we have lived through a shift in the paradigm of war. What has happened is that in the past, in what I call "industrial war," you sought to win a trial of strength and thereby break the will of your opponent, to finally dictate the result, the political outcome you wished to achieve. In our new paradigm, which I call "war amongst the people," you seek to change the intentions or capture the will of your opponent and the people amongst which you operate, to win the clash of wills and thereby win the trial of strength. The essential difference is that military force is no longer used to decide the political dispute, but rather to create a condition in which a strategic result is achieved.

In other words, violence is now a tool to shift popular support to achieve political ends rather than a tool to defeat other military forces. According to Smith, "War no longer exists."[8] Instead, physical violence or other antagonistic measures are varying in intensity but ubiquitous. This imagined new paradigm of war meshes with the second new theoretical paradigm: *unrestricted warfare*, or war without rules. This term emerged in a privately published 1999 book ostensibly authored by two senior Chinese military officers.[9] In it, they proposed that the only way to defeat the technology-dependent Americans would be to aggressively exploit measures short of war, including legal action, economic pressure, cyberattacks, and terrorism.[10] Unrestricted warfare is multidimensional and fine-tuned to achieve specific, targeted objectives. In an academic interpretation of unrestricted warfare,[11]

> [t]here are no rules; nothing is forbidden. [The United States encounters] a national security threat different from the conventional warfare for which we have become preeminent in the world. Adversaries employing unrestricted warfare use many modalities to create integrated attacks exploiting diverse areas of vulnerability in support of their grand strategy. Unrestricted warfare battlefields reach beyond the physical domain to include culture, information networks, economics and finance, natural resources and energy.

Steven Metz of the U.S. Army War College makes the case that Russia is propagating unrestricted warfare in eastern Europe.[12] Metz writes that the United States, bound by linear thinking and dated threshold paradigms, is particularly vulnerable to the aggressive, short-

---

[7] Rupert Smith as quoted in Toni Pfanner, "Interview with Sir General Rupert Smith," *International Review of the Red Cross*, Vol. 88, No. 864, December 2006, pp. 719–720.

[8] Rupert Smith, *The Utility of Force: The Art of War in the Modern World*, New York: Knopf, 2007, p. 3.

[9] Some experts doubt this document's authenticity. Whether or not two Chinese military officers actually wrote it, the document exists and has shaped Western debate over measures short of war.

[10] Qiao Liang and Wang Xiangsui, *Unrestricted Warfare*, Beijing: PLA Literature and Arts Publishing House, 1999.

[11] Johns Hopkins University Applied Physics Laboratory, "2009 Unrestricted Warfare Symposium," c. 2009.

[12] R. Smith, 2007; Robert Haddick, "The Civilianization of War," *National Interest*, April 11, 2014; Steven Metz, "In Ukraine, Russia Reveals Its Mastery of Unrestricted Warfare," *World Politics Review*, April 16, 2014. Smith also argues that the world is now in a continuous state of conflict and that old notions of periodic war and peace are inapplicable. One could argue that these old notions were never applicable in reality and that the world has always been in a state of conflict: The Cold War was, ostensibly, a period of peace between the United States and the Soviet Union.

of-war actions that Russian president Vladimir Putin has been willing to take in Crimea and eastern Ukraine.[13] Jason Heeg of the U.S. Department of Defense's (DoD's) Foreign Military Studies Office argues that China is putting the principles of unrestricted warfare into play in Latin America, Asia, and Africa as part of a broader policy of "economic imperialism."[14] And Iran's support of insurgents and its political actions in Iraq fits within the description of unrestricted warfare: Iran is applying limited resources to achieve specific objectives using various means and methods. Indeed, one could describe any action that any nation-state takes that falls short of high-order conventional or nuclear combat as unrestricted war.

But, although there are legitimate arguments within both the population-centric and unrestricted-warfare paradigms, we are not witness to a new paradigm of interstate conflict. *Current crises and tactics represent neither a revolution in geopolitics nor the emergence of a new generation of warfare.* Instead, the ways in which rival states are conceiving of and applying these traditional or technologically enhanced measures are increasingly sophisticated, non-linear, and difficult for the United States and its allies to counter with its own measures short of war.[15] What might be termed *conflict exhaustion* at the end of the Afghanistan and Iraq wars enhances the effectiveness of these measures against U.S. interests. But, although both timing and technology have enhanced rival effectiveness, neither the measures they have used nor the combinations of measures used are particularly novel.

War, War Among the People, Ideal War, Real War, Conflict, or Something Else?

A prima facie examination of post-9/11 conflict might make it appear that war among the people is more common than in the past. Of the many conflicts between 2001 and 2015, only the initial invasion of Iraq in 2003 neared the paradigm of traditional, conventional war, and even that was muddled by the use of non-conventional forces and combat in highly populated areas. But nation-states have applied force to change popular will, and specifically have applied force in and among civilian populations to obtain their objectives, for centuries. For every physically isolated set-piece battle, such as the massive desert combat at El Alamein, Egypt, in 1942, there have been as many or even more population-centric wars, such as the American Revolutionary War (1775–1783) and Philippine–American War (1899–1902).[16] Even a cursory

---

[13] See Paul K. Davis and Peter A. Wilson, *Looming Discontinuities in U.S. Military Strategy and Defense Planning: Colliding RMAs Necessitate a New Strategy*, Santa Monica, Calif.: RAND Corporation, OP-326-OSD, 2011, for a pre-2015 assessment of these potential threats.

[14] Jason Heeg, *Chinese Imperialism in 2013: Application of Unrestricted Warfare or the Legitimate Use of the Economic Instrument of National Power?* Fort Leavenworth, Kan.: Foreign Military Studies Office, September 29, 2013.

[15] *Measures short of war* is one of the more-generalizable terms used to address these kinds of activities. Others include but are not limited to *parawar, lawfare, subversion, coercion, asymmetry, compellance, pressure pointing, dominance, brinksmanship*, and *salami tactics*. This kind of activity is often described more simply as *politics* or *international relations*. Sometimes, terms for subordinate tactics, such as *covert action*, are used to address a much broader range of activities and political or economic policies.

[16] The *Caroline* case during the Canadian insurrections of 1837 exemplifies the long-standing use of war, and measures short of war, among the people. The *Caroline* was a civilian U.S. steamship harbored at Fort Schlosser, New York, just across the Niagara River and the international border with Canada. Against U.S. federal policy, the *Caroline* was used to ferry Canadian insurgent fighters across the river to stage for attacks against Canadian loyalist forces and their British backers. The commander of the British forces authorized a small team of British troops to cross the Niagara River and destroy the *Caroline*. The British attacked across the international boundary in small-boat teams, seized the *Caroline*, set it afire, adrift, and then downriver over the Niagara Falls before withdrawing back to the Canadian side of the border. The United States lodged complaints, but the British raid succeeded without significant political consequence or escalation to high-order war.

accounting of limited and high-order wars in the 19th and 20th centuries shows that war by and among the people has by far been the most common type of warfare. For example, the oft-cited 2003 Fearon–Laitin study of civil war determined that there were 25 interstate wars and 127 civil wars between 1945 and 1999, a roughly 1:5 ratio.[17]

And, although war among the people is the most common type of war, isolated set-piece war is still possible. Smith writes that the last "real" tank battle took place on the Golan Heights during the 1973 Arab–Israeli War.[18] Yet the Persian Gulf War (1991) is not ancient history, and, although the war was one-sided, it did consist of tanks fighting tanks (e.g., Battle of 73 Easting), infantry fighting infantry, and traditional artillery duels in an isolated desert environment.[19] Assuming the demise of any type of warfare is, at best, unwise: After the Vietnam War, most U.S. planners assumed that counterinsurgency was gone forever, and just over 20 years later, Afghanistan and Iraq proved that it was not.[20] And, although, in early 2014, it would have seemed impossible that the North Atlantic Treaty Organization (NATO) might enter into tank-on-tank, plane-on-plane conventional combat with Russia, this outcome seemed at least remotely possible as of mid-2015. Certainly, DoD holds to the idea that conventional war is not only possible but also a pressing threat: The "pivot-to-Asia" strategy; the acquisition of advanced aircraft, such as the F-22- and F-35-series fighter-bombers; and the continued procurement and employment of heavy armored vehicles show that conventional war—even if it is a complex conventional war—is still central to U.S. strategic thought.

Conflict today, therefore, can range from high-order isolated conventional combat, to irregular warfare, complex urban warfare, and to all measures short of war, just as it could in 1775, 1837, and 1942. Further, the idea that war (or, more broadly, interstate conflict) is a contest of political wills designed to change popular support is central to long-standing tenets. Carl von Clausewitz described *ideal war* as combat removed from all other inputs, such as refugees or political corruption, yet most interpretations of his work show that Clausewitz viewed *ideal war* as strictly theoretical.[21] Clausewitz's *real war* was war situated in reality with all of the incumbent mess and complexity of human interaction. Real war was a contest of wills designed to change political behavior, and war was sublimated to political objectives; warfare was a tool to change political behavior. Rupert Smith stated that the distinction between

---

For brief accounts of this action, see, for example, L. N. Fuller, "British Steamer Is Burned by the Patriots," in *Northern New York in the Patriot War*, Watertown, N.Y.: Brockway Company, 1923; Hunter Miller, ed., "The Caroline," *Treaties and Other International Acts of the United States of America*, Vol. 4: *Documents 80–121*, Washington, D.C.: Government Printing Office, 1934, pp. 1836–1846; and Louis-Philippe Rouillard, "The Caroline Case: Anticipatory Self-Defence in Contemporary International Law," *Miskolc Journal of International Law*, Vol. 1, No. 2, 2004, pp. 104–120. Fuller recounts "river pirate" William Johnston's burning of the British steamer *Sir Robert Peel* in retaliation for the burning of the *Caroline*. This unofficial response might have been the only act of violence directly consequent to the British raid.

[17] *Interstate war* roughly corresponds to "high-order" war, and *civil war* roughly corresponds to Smith's war among the people.

[18] R. Smith, 2007, p. 3.

[19] For example, see H. R. McMaster, *Battle of 73 Easting*, U.S. Army, undated.

[20] Counterinsurgency disappeared from most U.S. military doctrine and had to be fully reexamined as a warfighting strategy for the wars in Afghanistan (2001–2015) and Iraq (2003–2011).

[21] This report does not claim to resolve all disputes over Clausewitz's theories. For a basic interpretation of the distinction between ideal war and real war, see Christopher Bassford, *Clausewitz and His Works*, March 18, 2013.

"industrial war" and "war amongst the people" was that, in the latter, violence was used to set the conditions for political change.[22] It is not at all clear how these are distinct from each other.

Although Rupert Smith does not identify anything new, he presents a useful mélange of various long-standing realist views of international relations. Smith's state of constant conflict mirrors the realist precept of international anarchy. Various schools of realism describe this differently, but, at its core, realism views interstate relations through the lens of unregulated and practical self-interest. This now oft-contested idea of interstate anarchy resides in various forms at the core of realist treatises on international relations, including those of Thucydides, Thomas Hobbes, Niccolò Machiavelli, and, more recently, Hans Morgenthau, George Kennan, Herman Kahn, Kenneth Waltz, and Gideon Rose.[23] Many classical and neoclassical realists argue that unregulated, or at least informally negotiated, interstate conflict is continuously played out at many levels and in varying degrees of intensity over time and space. Sometimes, it is nascent or covert; at other times, it is overt. Nation-states, such as Russia, China, Iran, and the United States, are designed to prosecute and defend against war and methods short of war within this state of conflict. Since 2001, the United States simply has not defended against methods short of war with sufficient flexibility or effectiveness to prevent threshold stretching and exploitation.

Restricted Unrestricted Warfare

This brings us to the theoretical paradigm of *unrestricted warfare*. This is an unfortunate term in that it can be easily misinterpreted. First, the term *unrestricted* creates the false impression that nation-states prosecuting unrestricted warfare can and will do whatever they want to achieve any objective desired. This might lead to absolute or total war, which Clausewitz and others described as abject violence without any limits on scope, scale, or means.[24] At the nation-state level, this kind of unrealistic and unlikely "all-in, all-the-way" behavior would lead almost immediately to full-scale nuclear conflict, which, in turn, would leave any survivors living in a postapocalyptic social, economic, and security wasteland. Clearly, this is not what the champions of the term *unrestricted warfare* have in mind. Second, *unrestricted warfare* is not intended to describe what is traditionally called *warfare*. Instead of describing large-scale, force-on-force combat, it more typically encompasses the murkiest, least physically violent, or smallest-scale violent measures short of war, such as cyberattacks and terrorism. When interpreted as its proponents intend it, the term *unrestricted warfare* describes strategies and tactics that are neither unrestricted nor warfare.

---

[22] Rupert Smith as quoted in Pfanner, 2006, pp. 719–720.

[23] Hans J. Morgenthau, *Politics Among Nations: The Struggle for Power and Peace*, New York: A. A. Knopf, 1948; Hans J. Morgenthau, "The Four Paradoxes of Nuclear Strategy," *American Political Science Review*, Vol. 58, No. 1, March 1964, pp. 23–35; George F. Kennan, "Inauguration of Organized Political Warfare," Washington, D.C.: Foreign Relations of the United States, 1945–1950, Retrospective Volume, Emergence of the Intelligence Establishment, Policy Planning Staff Memorandum, Document 269, May 4, 1948; Herman Kahn, *On Thermonuclear War*, Princeton, N.J.: Princeton University Press, 1960; Kenneth N. Waltz, "Nuclear Myths and Political Realities," *American Political Science Review*, Vol. 84, No. 3, September 1990, pp. 731–745; Gideon Rose, "Review: Neoclassical Realism and Theories of Foreign Policy," *World Politics*, Vol. 51, No. 1, October 1998, pp. 144–172; Jeffrey W. Legro and Andrew Moravcsik, "Is Anybody Still a Realist?" *International Security*, Vol. 24, No. 2, Fall 1999, pp. 5–55; Jack Donnelly, *Realism and International Relations*, Cambridge, UK: Cambridge University Press, 2000.

[24] The terms *absolute* and *total* war are both attributed and misattributed to Clausewitz. The attributions might or might not be accurate, but the meaning here is simple: complete warfare without limit.

More-specific interpretations of *unrestricted warfare* help explain its meaning. Ronald R. Luman, the director of Johns Hopkins University's National Security Analysis Department and the Unrestricted Warfare Symposium, proposes this more-reasonable interpretation: "The chief characteristic of unrestricted warfare is unrestricted use of measures, not unrestricted strategies or objectives."[25]

In other words, nation-states (and nonstate actors) are now more likely to use any and all measures short of war available to achieve their strategic objectives, but they will use these measures in a way that sensibly weighs risk with reward. This is clear, logical, and anchored in evidence-tested theory. Both war and the use of methods short of war are unregulated, but some norms and practicalities *generally* guide international behavior. Barring total domination of a national political and military leadership by psychopaths, nations are *likely* to restrict their actions to avoid what they perceive to be near-certain destruction or because they see insufficient advantage in high-order war.[26] There are very practical reasons that Russia did not launch a nuclear attack against the United States during the Cold War and did not roll armored columns into Kiev in 2014, that China has not conducted unrestricted cyberattacks against the United States, and that Iran has not murdered all Israeli or U.S. citizens within the reach of its Quds Force operatives. Although all three countries aggressively exploit loopholes or gray areas in local treaties and international law, they most often behave in a way that signals recognition of practical restrictions.

What, then, is *unrestricted war* in practice? According to the Chinese book and a range of Western interpretations, *unrestricted warfare* is no more than the focused and aggressive use of measures short of war to achieve limited strategic ends. Unrestricted war takes advantage of changing technology and includes actions in cyberspace; otherwise, it consists of a focused mixture of terrorism, economic pressure, covert action, enabling proxies, and political and legal action. Other than cyberwarfare, none of these methods is new. As we described above, all of these methods have been used extensively, aggressively, and in ingenious combinations by most nation-states throughout the course of history.[27] *Unrestricted warfare* is, at worst, misleading and, at best, a contemporary catchphrase for long-standing international practice.

Threshold Exploitation and Stretching

Instead of prosecuting unrestricted war among the people, Russia, China, and Iran have simply taken successful or serendipitous risks that have resulted in expense to U.S. prestige and regional influence. Arguably, they perceive that the United States is increasingly reluctant to fight in the wake of the wars in Afghanistan and Iraq. Although they have taken some risk, each of these competitors appears to have identified U.S. and allied *thresholds* for war in very

---

[25] Ronald R. Luman, ed., *Unrestricted Warfare Symposium 2009: Proceedings on Combating the Unrestricted Warfare Threat—Terrorism, Resources, Economics, and Cyberspace*, Laurel, Md.: Johns Hopkins University Applied Physics Laboratory, 2009, p. 2.

[26] See the recent work on prospect theory for deeper discussions of this dynamic. Nearly all the realist literature, and much of the antirealist literature, also addresses rational assumptions of decisionmaking. This *is not* to say that we assume or propose that all decisionmaking is rational, predictable, and individualistic; these issues are hotly contested in both theory and in analyses of large-sample-size case studies. Instead, we argue only that, in most cases, international decisionmaking is more practical and risk-conscious than wildly and unthinkingly aggressive.

[27] Some measures are used more often or more directly by some states than others, and some states lack the capacity or political support to employ certain measures. North Korea cannot successfully apply economic sanctions against South Korea or the United States, and the United States is unlikely to support international terrorism against civilians.

specific local situations or exploited the gray areas in tacitly derived thresholds. Each of these rivals has applied a contextualized and well-tailored mix of pinpoint economic and political pressure, surprising bursts of overt but limited power projection, and a range of covert or indirect measures. Sometimes, these efforts appear to be part of a carefully orchestrated, long-range national plan, while others might constitute a mix of shorter-term, ad hoc tactics. In some cases, such as the 2014 shooting down of Malaysia Airlines flight MH17, they are reckless or at least poorly considered and controlled.[28] Nonetheless, the results are at least tactically effective and strategically troubling.

Rollbacks in Ukraine, east Asia, and the Middle East indicate that the United States is increasingly vulnerable to what might be termed *threshold stretching* or *threshold exploitation* and that, below the level of massive, overt economic sanctions, it lacks policies, strategies, and response options to counter these approaches. Russia, China, and Iran have not only exploited war thresholds; they have also arguably redefined them by applying finely tuned pressure against U.S. and allied strategic soft spots. Further, it is not clear that the United States has developed or thoughtfully integrated corresponding or even more-effective ways and means to exploit rival thresholds. Any U.S. measures short of war must comply with U.S. and many international laws, so nations that are less concerned with legal limitations might have at least an inherent tactical advantage. This gap places the United States and its allies at a strategic disadvantage that, over time, might contribute to the global rollback of U.S. influence and power.

This report spotlights the trends of threshold stretching and exploitation and provides insights from three recent examples: Russia and Ukraine, China in the East China Sea, and Iran in Iraq. It identifies a dangerous gap between U.S. strategic thought and policy and rival strategies and policy, and it recommends research questions designed to address, and redress, this gap.

---

[28] Flight MH17 was ostensibly shot down by a Russian-made surface-to-air missile in the hands of Ukrainian separatists.

CHAPTER TWO

American Understanding of Thresholds Is Impractical

Just as the so-called new paradigms of war are misleading, so are the enduring American assumptions of linear escalation and enduring thresholds. Some of the most influential official and academic interpretations of U.S. strategic thought are at once dated and historically misleading: They (probably unintentionally) gave the impression that Cold War strategy consisted almost entirely of conventional and nuclear threshold calculation when in fact it consisted primarily of proxy wars and the common, brutal, and aggressive use of measures short of war. These official and academic interpretations also lead one to believe that "things have changed" since the terror attacks of 9/11 and that, between nation-states, the Marquess of Queensberry rules of the Cold War no longer apply. In fact, these linear rules for the application of power or the escalation of force never applied outside of grand theory.

Based on their Cold War experiences, Kennan and other venerated experts on nation-state power and use of force tended to situate measures short of war within a linear sequence, or scale, in which each measure moved actors closer to the threshold of high-order conventional or nuclear war. Powerful conventionally and nuclear-armed states, such as the Soviet Union or the United States, might avoid war by applying only those measures that stopped below known thresholds. Herman Kahn built the most noted of these simplified linear scales.[1] It consists of a sequential series of 44 rungs, or steps, from very low-level political maneuvering to "insensate war," which is equivalent to unrestricted nuclear combat.[2] Figure 2.1 is an exemplified version of Kahn's escalation ladder, developed in the wake of the Cuban Missile and Berlin crises of the early 1960s. Because the threat of nuclear war drove Kahn's Cold War analysis, his critical threshold lies between maneuvering and crises on one hand and "central wars"—or war including the use of many nuclear weapons—on the other.

Although the simplifications in linear sequencing theory were adequate to help U.S. decisionmakers avoid high-order conventional or nuclear combat during the Cold War, they are inadequate to explain and plan for such events as the Russian seizure of Crimea.[3] Linear escalation assumes that nation-state thresholds for high-order war are known and relatively fixed and that escalation occurs mostly in detectable, ordinal steps. Even during the Cold War, this

---

[1] Herman Kahn, *On Escalation: Metaphors and Scenarios*, New York: Praeger, 1965.

[2] Kahn, 1965, p. 39.

[3] Kahn was a careful scholar, and *On Escalation* is laden with caveats. He clearly understood that the ladder was a theoretical simplification, and he explicitly stated that it should not be used to formulate real policy. He describes the ladder as an "archetype" and writes, "escalation ladders are metaphorical tools that have been found useful in preliminary studies of escalation. No particular ladder should be considered as . . . a theory of international relations" (Kahn, 1965, p. 38). However, Kahn's ladder was indeed used to formulate strategy and clearly had some influence on the development of the U.S. doctrine of Flexible Response.

Figure 2.1
Herman Kahn's Escalation Ladder

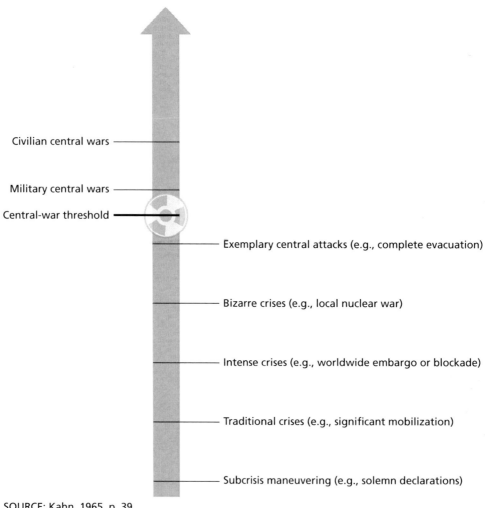

Civilian central wars

Military central wars

Central-war threshold

Exemplary central attacks (e.g., complete evacuation)

Bizarre crises (e.g., local nuclear war)

Intense crises (e.g., worldwide embargo or blockade)

Traditional crises (e.g., significant mobilization)

Subcrisis maneuvering (e.g., solemn declarations)

SOURCE: Kahn, 1965, p. 39.
RAND RR1003-2.1

was an unrealistic assumption: Both the United States and the Soviet Union identified thresholds for the use of nuclear war, but it is doubtful that these thresholds accurately reflected policymaker viewpoints or authorities over time. For example, although the United States had a formal doctrine for laddered escalation against prospective Soviet aggression called Flexible Response, there is significant evidence that U.S. policymakers never incorporated Flexible Response into strategic or operational assumptions or planning. NATO allies only reluctantly incorporated Flexible Response into doctrine and then essentially ignored the concept until it faded away.[4]

---

[4]   See Francis J. Gavin, "The Myth of Flexible Response: United States Strategy in Europe During the 1960s," *International History Review*, Vol. 23, No. 4, December 2001, pp. 847–855. Also see J. Michael Legge, *Theater Nuclear Weapons and the NATO Strategy of Flexible Response*, Santa Monica, Calif.: RAND Corporation, R-2964-FF, 1983. One reviewer of this report noted that the doctrine of Flexible Response was simply too expensive for NATO implementation.

And as Kahn, Paul Pillar, and others have made clear, thresholds have and will continue to have different meaning in different places at different times.[5] Although the United States has expressed its willingness to invoke Article 5 of the Washington treaty and go to high-order war to defend NATO allies' homelands, as recently as the late 20th century, the United States has been unwilling to invoke Article 5 and provide overt military aid to help NATO allies defend various colonial outposts.[6] For example, the United States did not provide overt military aid to the United Kingdom during the Falkland Islands War in 1982 despite the fact that the United Kingdom claimed the Falklands as sovereign territory.[7] Unwillingness to commit force also applies to nonstated but widely assumed thresholds, such as those tied to U.S. rhetorical intolerance for genocide or other humanitarian crises.[8] Although President Bill Clinton did step in to help curtail genocide in the Balkans in the 1990s, he did not respond to genocide in Rwanda in the same decade. Timing plays a critical role in this kind of decisionmaking. Perhaps the actions of Syrian president Bashar al-Assad against his people might have triggered an overt U.S. or NATO military response if they had occurred prior to the exhausting Afghanistan and Iraq wars, but, as of mid-2015, the United States had not responded in force to Syrian war crimes, including the reported use of chemical weapons. Written or stated thresholds can, in fact, be conscious bluffs, or policymakers might simply lack the willpower or inclination to react to threshold crossing at any one time—or in any specific location—for any number of reasons.[9]

Thomas C. Schelling, a contemporary of Kahn, offered a different take on thresholds and limited war. In a series of publications in the 1950s and 1960s, Schelling argued that many thresholds for high-order war were defined not by negotiation or firm public statement but by tacit bargains that were mutually beneficial to all sides.[10] Schelling applied his interpretation of game theory and heuristics to the gray area between measures short of war and high-order war, and to "limited war," or war short of total national annihilation.[11] Competing nation-states find themselves in a continuous state of implicit negotiation, feeling out each others' perceptions, willpower, and capabilities regarding war thresholds. Uncertainty and inaccuracy are endemic, yet, in most cases, nation-states find a mutually beneficial compromise. Schelling offers many compelling examples, including the nonuse of the prodigious stores of chemical weapons held by both Axis and Allied powers during World War II. Yet Schelling emphasized points of agreement rather than the dangerous miscalculations and inherent ambiguities in

---

[5] Kahn, 1965; Paul R. Pillar, "The Forgotten Principles of Deterrence," *National Interest*, March 28, 2014.

[6] Article 5 has been invoked only once: in response to the 2001 terror attacks against the United States. For a brief description and discussion of Article 5, see NATO, "What Is Article 5?" undated.

[7] The United States provided intelligence support to the United Kingdom during the Falkland Islands War.

[8] Public statements by U.S. political leaders and national security documents, such as those cited later in this chapter, periodically reinforce these assumptions.

[9] In some cases, they could react with countervailing measures short of war, and some of these might be hidden from public view. However, strategic setbacks are typically visible to all, and judgments of strategic failure are typically well defended and even publicly stated by U.S. officials. For example, President Clinton publicly acknowledged his failure to react to the genocide in Rwanda ("Bill Clinton: We Could Have Saved 3,000 Lives in Rwanda," CNBC, March 13, 2013).

[10] See, e.g., Thomas C. Schelling, "An Essay on Bargaining," *American Economic Review*, Vol. 46, No. 3, June 1956, pp. 281–306; Thomas C. Schelling, "Bargaining, Communication, and Limited War," *Conflict Resolution*, Vol. 1, No. 1, March 1957, pp. 19–36; Thomas C. Schelling, *Arms and Influence*, New Haven, Conn.: Yale University Press, 1966.

[11] Schelling, 1957, p. 19.

tacitly achieved thresholds. This emphasis perhaps contributed to the unhelpful notion that thresholds were and are more imperturbable than murky and often misunderstood.

Dominant realist theorists and practitioners intentionally and sometimes unintentionally encouraged acceptance of these conveniently neat linear models. Various incarnations or interpretations of realism governed nearly all Western strategic thought from the mid–20th century through mid-2015. Kahn, Schelling, Morgenthau, and Kennan were influenced by and, in turn, influenced other prominent realists and had both direct and indirect input into U.S. national strategy. The most prominent and influential senior advisers to post–World War II U.S. presidents have, arguably, been overtly or quietly realist in their outlooks.[12] Advances in modeling, heuristics, and the development of finely tuned quantitative tests, such as Bruce Bueno de Mesquita's rational-expectation approach, have reinforced the idea that national policy behavior can be accurately forecasted.[13] In his critiques of rational-expectation modeling, Stephen Walt argues that this "second wave" of realists has gone too far in reducing complex realities into black-box equations that, in turn, undermine efforts to impress policymakers with the uncertainties inherent in decisionmaking and forecasting.[14] Bueno de Mesquita and others argue that rational-expectation or rational-choice modeling has greatly benefited both science and policy. Bueno de Mesquita suggests that his approach might give "lawlike knowledge" of war threshold calculations, and the U.S. government has used his models to forecast instability and war.[15] This report cannot and does not seek to resolve the debates over realism and rational-expectation modeling. Instead, it is enough to note that this Western imperative

---

[12] These include John Foster Dulles, Secretary of State under Dwight D. Eisenhower; Arthur M. Schlesinger, Jr., special assistant to John F. Kennedy; Robert S. McNamara, Secretary of Defense under Kennedy and Lyndon B. Johnson; Henry Kissinger, national security adviser and Secretary of State under Richard Nixon and Gerald Ford; Zbigniew K. Brzezinski, counselor to Johnson and national security adviser to Jimmy Carter; James Baker, Secretary of State under George H. W. Bush; George P. Shultz, Secretary of State under Reagan; Brent Scowcroft, national security adviser under Ford and George H. W. Bush, military assistant to Nixon, and Deputy Assistant to the President for National Security Affairs under Nixon and Ford; Madeleine Albright, Secretary of State under Bill Clinton; Dick Cheney, Secretary of Defense under George H. W. Bush and Vice President under George W. Bush; and Susan Rice, national security adviser under Barack Obama. Some advisers were self-described or labeled as idealist-realists, e.g., Anthony Lake during the Clinton presidency.

[13] This field also includes prospect theory and a wide range of debates over interpretations and relative values of risk, gain, and loss assumptions and calculations. See, e.g., Bruce Bueno de Mesquita, "The Costs of War: A Rational Expectations Approach," *American Political Science Review*, Vol. 77, No. 2, June 1983, pp. 347–357; Bruce Bueno de Mesquita, "Toward a Scientific Understanding of International Conflict: A Personal View," *International Studies Quarterly*, Vol. 29, No. 2, June 1985, pp. 121–136; Bruce Bueno de Mesquita and David Lalman, *War and Reason: Domestic and International Imperatives*, New Haven, Conn.: Yale University Press, 1992; Bruce Bueno de Mesquita and James D. Morrow, "Sorting Through the Wealth of Notions," *International Security*, Vol. 24, No. 2, Fall 1999, pp. 56–73; Bruce Bueno de Mesquita, James D. Morrow, Randolph M. Siverson, and Alastair Smith, "An Institutional Explanation of the Democratic Peace," *American Political Science Review*, Vol. 93, No. 4, December 1999, pp. 791–807; Stuart A. Bremer, "Dangerous Dyads: Conditions Affecting the Likelihood of Interstate War, 1816–1965," *Journal of Conflict Resolution*, Vol. 36, No. 2, June 1992, pp. 309–341; James D. Morrow, *Game Theory for Political Scientists*, Princeton, N.J.: Princeton University Press, 1995; Matthew Rabin, "Risk Aversion and Expected-Utility Theory: A Calibration Theorem," *Econometrica*, Vol. 68, No. 5, September 2000, pp. 1281–1292; Matthew Rabin and Richard H. Thaler, "Anomalies: Risk Aversion," *Journal of Economic Perspectives*, Vol. 15, No. 1, Winter 2001, pp. 219–232; Jack S. Levy, "Prospect Theory, Rational Choice, and International Relations," *International Studies Quarterly*, Vol. 41, No. 1, March 1997, pp. 87–112; Jonathan Kulick and Paul K. Davis, *Modeling Adversaries and Related Cognitive Biases*, Santa Monica, Calif.: RAND Corporation, RP-1084, 2003; and Duncan Snidal, "International Cooperation Among Relative Gains Maximizers," *International Studies Quarterly*, Vol. 35, No. 4, December 1991, pp. 387–402.

[14] Stephen M. Walt, "Rigor or Rigor Mortis? Rational Choice and Security Studies," *International Security*, Vol. 23, No. 4, Spring 1999, p. 4.

[15] Bueno de Mesquita, 1983, 1985; Bueno de Mesquita and Lalman, 1992.

to classify and rationalize international behavior has influenced the way U.S. policymakers approach the issue of thresholds.

Because thresholds are so fuzzy and complex and policymakers require surety, the kind of models that Kahn and others intended to remain theoretical were instead applied in both explicit and implicit ways over the course of the Cold War and into the early 21st century. These concepts took root as a broad strategic paradigm of escalation anchored against logical, pragmatic, yet imagined thresholds for high-order war. There is ample evidence of rational and often linear thinking in nearly all important U.S. national security documents published from the mid–20th to early 21st centuries, beginning with National Security Council (NSC) Paper 68 in 1950 and continuing through President Obama's 2015 guidance on U.S. defense priorities.[16] With few exceptions, all of the presidents' national security memoranda and strategies from the 1950s through 2014 are predicated on realism.[17] Although the most-recent strategic documents emphasize multinational partnerships, the practical elements of these strategies all assume some version of international anarchy.[18] The following is a sample of quotes from national security memoranda from the 1960s through the 2010s. Each quote is associated with a broad tenet or assumption inherent to most realist theories.[19]

> *On calculated risk and reward:* We should continue roughly the present slowly ascending tempo of Rolling Thunder [aerial bombing] operations, being prepared to add strikes [or] to slow the pace [in response to Vietcong actions].
> —*McGeorge Bundy, while national security adviser under President Johnson, 1965*[20]

---

[16] James S. Lay, Jr., *A Report to the National Security Council*, Washington, D.C.: National Security Council Paper 68, April 14, 1950; Barack Obama, *National Security Strategy*, Washington, D.C.: White House, February 2015.

[17] One notable exception is George W. Bush's 2006 National Security Strategy. That document incorporates many elements of realism but places strong emphasis on idealism. Both Presidents Carter and Reagan were described as idealists, but some realist limits guided Carter's human rights policy: "We do not seek to change governments or remake societies. Our experience in Vietnam and elsewhere [has] taught us the limits of our power" (Warren Christopher, "PRM on Human Rights," Washington, D.C.: Office of the Deputy Secretary of State, Presidential Review Memorandum/National Security Council Paper 28, July 8, 1977, p. 4). Reagan's strategic writings might have been anchored in idealistic language, but, even in public documents, such as the 1987 National Security Strategy, they were practical and clearly realist in their approaches.

[18] See, e.g., Ronald W. Reagan, *National Security Strategy of the United States*, Washington, D.C.: White House, 1987; George H. W. Bush, *National Security Strategy of the United States*, Washington, D.C.: White House, August 1, 1991; Bill Clinton, *A National Security Strategy of Engagement and Enlargement*, Washington, D.C.: White House, July 1, 1994; Bill Clinton, *A National Security Strategy for a New Century*, Washington, D.C.: White House, 1998; Barack Obama, *National Security Strategy*, Washington, D.C.: White House, May 27, 2010; Barack Obama, *Sustaining U.S. Global Leadership: Priorities for 21st Century Defense*, Washington, D.C.: White House, January 2012. For example, see Obama, 2010, p. 45:

> Wars over ideology have given way to wars over religious, ethnic, and tribal identity; nuclear dangers have proliferated; inequality and economic instability have intensified; damage to our environment, food insecurity, and dangers to public health are increasingly shared; and the same tools that empower individuals to build enable them to destroy.

[19] We examined a sample of relevant memoranda from the online library holdings of each president from Eisenhower through George W. Bush.

[20] McGeorge Bundy, untitled memorandum for the Secretary of State, the Secretary of Defense, and the Director of Central Intelligence, Washington, D.C.: White House, National Security Action Memorandum 328, April 6, 1965a, p. 2. This policy assumed that graduated pressure against the Vietcong and North Vietnam would elicit a desired and *equivalent* easing of pressure against the government and military of South Vietnam.

On expecting rational behavior: Maintain forces to insure [sic] that the Soviet Union would have no incentive to strike the United States first in a crisis.
—Henry Kissinger, while national security adviser and Secretary of State under President Nixon, 1969[21]

On calculated thresholds: [Failure to improve our nuclear capabilities] lowers the nuclear threshold.
—Donald H. Rumsfeld, while Secretary of Defense under President Ford[22]

On the balance of power: [T]he United States will maintain an overall balance of military power between the United States . . . and the Soviet Union. . . .
—President Carter, 1977[23]

On the balance of power: A key task for the future will be maintaining regional balances. . . .
—President George H. W. Bush, 1991[24]

On expecting rational behavior: Free governments do not . . . attack other free nations.
—President George W. Bush, 2006[25]

Arguably, the long-lasting overemphasis on linear, rationalist thinking—*intended or not by realist theorists*—encouraged a dangerously misleading set of assumptions to obtain in U.S. policy and in the development of operational capabilities. The first of these assumptions is that nation-state rivals, such as Russia, China, and Iran, *almost certainly* would not undertake certain actions. For example, Russia would prepare for but make all efforts to avoid even a limited armored attack in Europe because this escalation would cross the U.S. threshold of high-order—and perhaps nuclear—war. Buildup of NATO conventional and nuclear forces helped to reinforce this part-negotiated and part-tacit threshold. Second, nation-state rivals might conduct covert operations, but their overt actions would pay due respect to U.S. interpretations of international law. For example, China would not take the step of unilaterally expanding its airspace beyond widely accepted international limits. And third, nation-state rivals would not risk killing U.S. military personnel because this act would ostensibly constitute an act of war. For example, Russia, China, and Iran would not directly assist in killing U.S. forces.

---

[21] Henry A. Kissinger, "Criteria for Strategic Sufficiency," Washington, D.C.: National Security Council, National Security Decision Memorandum 16, June 24, 1969. This was one of four priorities for "strategic sufficiency" for U.S. nuclear policy.

[22] Jeanne W. Davis, "Minutes of NSC Meeting Held December 15, 1976," memorandum for Brent Scowcroft, Washington, D.C.: National Security Council, January 3, 1977, p. 6. Rumsfeld said this during an NSC meeting with President Ford in attendance.

[23] Jimmy Carter, "U.S. National Strategy," Washington, D.C.: White House, Presidential Directive/National Security Council Paper 18, August 26, 1977a, p. 2.

[24] G. H. W. Bush, 1991, p. 7.

[25] George W. Bush, *National Security Strategy of the United States of America*, Washington, D.C.: White House, March 2006.

Of course, all of these assumptions, and many others associated with theoretical escalation and threshold paradigms, have been and continue to be false.[26] They represent not only impractical or oversimplified international theory but also a range of cognitive biases that undermine effective strategy.[27] Assumptions of linear rationality feed a belief that all sides implicitly understand and respect even the most poorly defined thresholds for high-order war. Colin S. Gray argues that some of these problems, and the sometimes-dramatic swings between over- and underpreparation for high-order war, are endemic to U.S. strategic culture.[28] Whether or not this is always the case, these false (or at least mistaken) assumptions and biases have made the United States vulnerable to nation-state and nonstate actors who have recognized and taken advantage of inconsistencies, weaknesses, and outright gaps in U.S. national and regional policy. Although the United States successfully staved off high-order conventional and nuclear war with Russia, China, and Iran, it has often succumbed to measures short of war. Chapter Three details three critical and timely examples.

---

[26] Russia did conduct an armored invasion in Georgia and South Ossetia in 2008; China did unexpectedly expand its airspace in 2013; and all three countries have directly helped kill U.S. service members in proxy combat (e.g., Russian pilots fought U.S. pilots during the Korean War; Chinese advisers helped kill U.S. pilots and infantry during the Vietnam War; and Iranian advisers helped kill both U.S. military and civilian personnel in Iraq).

[27] See Kulick and Davis, 2003.

[28] Colin S. Gray, "National Style in Strategy: The American Example," *International Security*, Vol. 6, No. 2, Fall 1981, pp. 21–47. We note that Alastair Iain Johnston and others recommend caution when assessing strategic culture or openly question the validity of strategic culture as a valid theoretical basis for analysis (see, e.g., Alastair Iain Johnston, "Thinking About Strategic Culture," *International Security*, Vol. 19, No. 4, Spring 1995b, pp. 32–64).

CHAPTER THREE

Russia, China, and Iran Apply Measures Short of War

This chapter presents three examples of the use of measures short of war to exploit and stretch thresholds for high-order war. Each of these scenarios continues to evolve as this report goes to publication, so some information might be dated. However, insight into the strategic thinking and procedures that Russia, China, and Iran demonstrate even in the incipient phases of each case has enduring value.

Example 1: Russia Exploits and Stretches Thresholds in Eastern Europe

Since the revolt that overthrew the Ukrainian government in early 2014, Russia appears to have executed a deliberate and systematic campaign to seize or indirectly control Ukrainian territory and to destabilize the interim Ukrainian government. Although the Russian plan to seize Crimea might have been quickly cobbled together, the speed and boldness of Russian action in Ukraine suggests that Putin and his various staffs had previously identified a deep vulnerability in U.S. and NATO regional policies and capabilities. As of mid-2015, neither the United States nor its allies had clearly stated policy interests in Ukraine, nor did they present a clear threshold for war if Russia violated Ukraine's sovereignty. Russia's use of measures carefully calibrated not to elicit a NATO response in Georgia in 2008 and in Ukraine in 2014 has established unequivocal precedent for Russian intervention in countries that formerly belonged to the Russian-led Soviet Union. If any U.S. threshold for war in eastern Europe did exist, it might now have been exploited and stretched to the point that it is more amenable to Russian hegemonic ambitions than to supporting U.S. and European strategic interests. If that threshold did not exist in the minds of U.S. policymakers, it is not yet clear whether or how they have reconsidered it.

Putin might not have had the confidence to intervene in Ukraine had he not succeeded so brilliantly in Georgia and South Ossetia in 2008.[1] By baiting Georgian president Mikheil Saakashvili to overreach and attack South Ossetia in the opening moves of conflict, Putin was able to create sufficient legal justification to repulse and then severely punish Georgian military forces. Whether or not the Russian strategy in South Ossetia and Georgia resulted from rational long-range planning, the strategy worked. Russia leveraged the pro-Russian independence

---

[1] For details on the Russia–Georgia conflict and discussions of the legal justifications for Russian action, see Jim Nichol, *Russia–Georgia Conflict in August 2008: Context and Implications for U.S. Interests*, Washington, D.C.: Congressional Research Service, RL34618, March 3, 2009; and Nicolai N. Petro, "Legal Case for Russian Intervention in Georgia," *Fordham International Law Journal*, Vol. 32, No. 5, May 2009, pp. 1524–1549. We draw this summary from these sources, as well as from contemporary media reports on the conflict.

movement in South Ossetia to send first peacekeepers and then conventional military forces into the region. When Georgia attacked South Ossetia, the Russians responded with both overt military force and a range of covert actions, including cyberattacks against Georgian networks. Russian forces then executed a partial withdrawal and formalized their control of South Ossetia.

Why did the United States not respond to Russia's actions with military force? The United States did have interests in Georgia in 2008. Saakashvili was a Western-leaning leader, Georgia is in a remote yet potentially important location between Russia and NATO member Turkey, and the Georgian military had deployed forces in support of the U.S.-led coalition in Iraq.[2] Yet, through 2008, Georgia was not a NATO member and was not protected by Article 5 of the Washington treaty that established NATO. Nor was Georgia a member of the European Union. The United States had no bilateral defense agreement with Georgia, and no U.S. leader had made firm public statements that the seizure of South Ossetia or military attacks into Georgian territory would be met with force. There was little legal standing for U.S. counter-intervention in Georgia. Further, in 2008, the wars in Afghanistan and Iraq distracted the United States; there was no political will to support military action in support of a non–NATO member. And although Georgia has some strategic significance, U.S. leaders probably consider it far less significant than dozens of other countries that require extensive U.S. attention.[3] Russia successfully gauged the likelihood of U.S. or NATO military response and changed the borders of eastern Europe in its favor. And although the United States provided aid to Georgia in the wake of the conflict, the lack of U.S. action there might have resonated with Russian leadership.

The political events preceding Russia's seizure of the Crimean Peninsula almost certainly provided the proximate cause, and the alacrity with which it was accomplished indicates that *some* prior planning had been done. It is not clear that Russia had the Georgia operation in mind when it decided to seize part of Ukraine, but the precedent would have been important. Whatever the case, its intervention was swift and seemed carefully calculated to avoid crossing U.S. or NATO thresholds for military response. Russian *tactics* (methods) used in Ukraine appear to have been well integrated and sophisticated. Russian *strategy* (overall approach) in Ukraine has undeniable parallels to its strategy in Georgia. However, use of these measures short of war was also redolent of Soviet Cold War tactics and, more deeply, a Soviet-era understanding of world history, power, and diplomacy. In the mid-1940s, the Soviets published a detailed, multivolume study of European diplomatic history that described nation-state behavior as fundamentally devious, opportunistic, and brutal.[4] It portrayed all capitalist states as purely Machiavellian. It described the Soviet state as the defender of peace and democracy and not at all devious.[5] Ironically, some of the sections on capitalist behavior read like a recipe book for the Soviet approach to international relations from the mid–20th century through 1989. These are translated section headings in the chapter on bourgeois methods of diplomacy: "The

---

[2]   See Dan Lamothe, "Marines to Extend Georgia Training Mission," *Marine Corps Times*, April 6, 2011.

[3]   We base this assessment on an informal review of U.S. strategic interests and the relevance of other countries in relation to Georgia. It is not derived from empirical analysis or from official U.S. government documents.

[4]   V. P. Potëmkin, ed., *Istoriia diplomati*, Moskva: Gos. sotsial'no-ekon. izd.-vo, 1941–1945, cited in C. E. Black, "Diplomatic History: The Soviet Approach—A Review Article," *American Slavic and East European Review*, Vol. 7, No. 3, October 1948, pp. 276–288.

[5]   Black, 1948.

Use of Pacifist Propaganda for the Purpose of Disorienting the Adversary," "The Propaganda for the So-Called Localization of Conflicts with the Disguised Purpose of Making It Easier for the Aggressor to Complete the Destruction of His Intended Victim," "The Method of Systematic Threats and of Terrorization of the Adversary," and "The So-Called Defense of Weak States as a Pretext for Aggression."[6]

Kennan argues that a few Soviet leaders might have genuinely embraced the fiction of a wholesome, altruistic Soviet state for a time. But World War II snapped them out of their reverie. By the late 1940s, the Soviets had reversed course and openly embraced "imperialistic" measures short of war as a means to avoid costly high-order combat.[7] Pretenses of idealism gave way to a hard-bitten realism. In addition to adopting policies of "deceptiveness and divisiveness" (capitalizing on existing military *maskirovka*, or camouflage and deception tactics), the Soviets were also cautious and flexible.[8] They planned for multiple courses of action and were fickle in their pursuit of objectives; they could pursue options or abandon them at will. Putin, a product of the Soviet education, political, diplomatic, and intelligence systems, applied all of these principles in Ukraine. In the early stages of the campaign, the Russians used propaganda to establish their peaceful, localized, and protective purposes, then they issued threats, and then they leveraged the image of vulnerable ethnic Russians to seize Crimea.[9]

The Russian operation in Crimea consisted of a masterful combination of graduated covert and overt tactics. By reportedly deploying special operations forces, some conventional troops, and irregulars in unmarked uniforms, the Russian military was able to create just enough doubt and confusion to delay a response; in short order, the presence of Russian special forces on Ukrainian soil became the new normal.[10] Evidence that the U.S. government substantiates indicates that Russia also sent in small groups of advisers to instigate and support pro-Russian militia forces in the Crimea, and it appears that at least some of the "militia" troops are, in fact, Russian special forces soldiers.[11] Over the course of a month, Russia gained incremental control over various parts of Crimea and leveraged pro-Russian Crimean politicians to bring about Crimean secession from Ukraine. Russia quickly followed up with a parliamentary vote that recognized Crimean independence and established Crimea as a de facto Russian protectorate. The entire operation was supported by an aggressive cyber- and media campaign that blocked or censored Ukrainian media outlets and utilized misinformation to discredit rivals. One columnist believed that the Russian propaganda campaign had been "breathtaking, even by Soviet standards."[12]

---

[6] Kennan, 1991, p. 63.

[7] These included but were not limited to "persuasion, intimidation, deceit, corruption, penetration, subversion, horse-trading, bluffing, psychological pressure, economic pressure, seduction, blackmail, theft, fraud, rape, battle, murder, and sudden death" (Kennan, 1991, p. 8).

[8] Kennan, 1991, p. 61; Kenneth C. Keating, Maskirovka: *The Soviet System of Camouflage*, Garmisch, Germany: U.S. Army Russian Institute, 1981.

[9] For a quick summary of events, see "Ukraine Crisis: Timeline," *BBC News*, November 13, 2014; or "Timeline: Ukraine's Political Crisis," *Aljazeera*, September 20, 2014.

[10] It helped that the Ukrainian government was also in a state of chaos at this point in time.

[11] See, e.g., Michael R. Gordon and Andrew E. Kramer, "Scrutiny over Photos Said to Tie Russia Units to Ukraine," *New York Times*, April 22, 2014.

[12] Celestine Bohlen, "Cold War Media Tactics Fuel Ukraine Crisis," *New York Times*, March 10, 2014.

Russia cannot completely control the outcome of the 2014–2015 Ukraine crisis. By June 2014, pro-Russian nationalists were taking risks that the Russians did not account for. Western economic sanctions, coupled with a seemingly serendipitous drop in oil prices, might be causing significant damage to the Russian economy. And although the Russian covert actions were effective, they were not flawless: Ubiquitous social media made it impossible to conceal the identity of Russian covert-action officers and special operations forces. No covert action or military operation can escape the inevitability of happenstance, individual failure, or the unpredictable behavior of opponents, but Russia set a new standard for threshold exploitation in Ukraine. In doing so, it has reshaped—or perhaps *reset*—both the regional and global understanding of U.S. power and influence.

The strategic implications of this reset are significant. Two of the guiding principles of U.S.–European security relations—namely, that Europe was stable ("whole and free") and that Russia could be a stabilizing influence and perhaps eventually a trusted partner—were destroyed.[13] It is still not clear whether the United States has a threshold for high-order war in Ukraine. It needs new policies and options for responding to acts of aggression calibrated to fall below the level of overt military action.

Example 2: China Expands Its Boundaries in East Asia

In the past several years, China has taken increasingly assertive action to defend and, arguably, to expand its exclusive economic zone and territorial water claims in the East and South China Seas.[14] In 2012, China was able to pressure the Philippine coast guard into withdrawing from a protracted standoff with its Chinese counterparts over the Scarborough Reef in the South China Sea. China and the Philippines are now in contention over the Second Thomas Shoal in the Spratly Islands. In 2013, China established an air defense identification zone (ADIZ) over much of the East China Sea as part of its ongoing effort to take full control of the Japanese-administered Senkaku Islands. This simple announcement sought to expand Chinese airspace beyond internationally recognized territory, though its efficacy remains in question. China is also pressing its claims for the Paracel Islands, which Vietnam claims as well.

The United States has no territorial claims to any of these island chains, but U.S. regional allies, such as the Philippines and Japan, view Chinese actions as threats to their national sovereignty. The United States has bilateral security agreements with both countries. Further, the United States is keenly interested in maintaining freedom of navigation in international airspace and waterways for both military and commercial vessels. For decades, the Chinese People's Liberation Army (PLA) has been aggressive in its attempts to deter U.S. military presence along its international air and sea boundaries. Controlling key archipelagos from Borneo to the Russian Kamchatka Peninsula would effectively extend Chinese territorial presence from the 12-mile international boundary and the 200-mile United Nations Convention on the Law of the Sea exclusive economic zone to hundreds of nautical miles out from the Chinese mainland

---

[13] We thank F. Stephen Larrabee of the RAND Corporation for this insight.

[14] Chinese officials might describe perceived expansions as simple reinforcement of existing territorial claims.

along a bending path from east of the Chinese coast to the distant south-southeast.[15] Chinese actions in the East and South China Seas are emblematic of China's broader strategy.

China and Japan have disputed the Senkaku Islands for centuries, but China has accelerated its efforts to gain total control over the islands in the past decade after Japan purchased the islands from a private owner. In November 2013, China established an ADIZ over the East China Sea, placing the islands under Chinese airspace. The ADIZ is now patrolled by PLA Air Force aircraft and law enforcement boats; these patrols are clearly intended to add weight to the ADIZ expansion and to set precedent for expanded Chinese military presence in the East China Sea. The United States and Japan have both declined to respect the declared ADIZ. Shortly after the announcement, the United States sent two B-52s through the zone.[16] Since 1960, the United States has asserted that the 1960 U.S.–Japan treaty[17] covers the Senkaku Islands; however, the United States takes no position on ownership of the islands. This latest action raises the question of why the U.S.–Japan security alliance is insufficient to deter China from expanding its territorial control in the East China Sea.

Since the 1960s, China has substantially and effectively grown the PLA and greatly expanded its economic power. At the same time, the Japanese Self-Defense Forces (SDF) have remained stagnant under Article 9 of the Japanese constitution, and, since the early 1990s, Japanese economic power and influence have ebbed. This shift in the balance of power in the East China Sea engendered Chinese nationalist expectations and presented opportunities for China to press its claims. China came out of the 2008 financial crisis relatively unscathed, while the United States did not.[18] Many analysts observed that China went through a particularly "assertive" period from 2008 to 2010.[19] Both Japan and the United States have taken significant measures to counterbalance China's increasing aggressiveness.[20] In 2010, Japan embarked on a program of continuing defense reform, shifting from its "basic defense force" doctrine to a new "dynamic defense force" construct better suited to countering Chinese influence in the East China Sea. Japan expanded its fiscal year 2013 defense budget, the first such expansion in 11 years. In September 2012, Japanese SDF and the U.S. Marine Corps conducted their first joint training designed to practice and demonstrate the ability to defend or reinforce remote islands and improve SDF amphibious capabilities.[21] However, none of these activities prevented China's establishment of the ADIZ in November 2013.

---

[15] This estimate is based on plotted direct-line distances between points along the Chinese coast and each of the island chains described in this report. For example, the distance from Guanyinjiao, China (N 27°22′28.07″, E 120°38′47.71″) to the Senkaku Island chain is approximately 180 nautical miles, while the distance from Dongchongcun, China (N 22°29′28.08″, E 114°34′45.49″) to the Scarborough Reef is approximately 470 nautical miles, and the distance from Li'anzhen, China (N 18°25′41.41″, E 110°4′11.83″) to the Spratly Islands is approximately 570 nautical miles. We approximated distances using the Google Earth linear ruler tool.

[16] Simon Denyer and Chico Harlan, "China Sends Warplanes to Patrol New Air Defense Zone," *Washington Post*, November 29, 2013.

[17] Treaty of Mutual Cooperation and Security Between Japan and the United States of America, January 19, 1960.

[18] Alastair Iain Johnston, *Cultural Realism: Strategic Culture and Grand Strategy in Chinese History*, Princeton, N.J.: Princeton University Press, 1995a; Dingding Chen, Xiaoyu Pu, and Alastair Iain Johnston, "Correspondence: Debating China's Assertiveness," *International Security*, Vol. 38, No. 3, Winter 2013–2014.

[19] Andrew Scobell and Scott Warren Harold, "An 'Assertive' China? Insights from Interviews," *Asian Security*, Vol. 9, No. 2, 2013, pp. 111–131; see Johnston, 1995a, for dissenting analysis.

[20] Ernesto Londoño, "Ahead of Beijing Visit, Defense Secretary Hagel Admonishes China," *Washington Post*, April 6, 2014.

[21] Kirk Spitzer, "U.S. and Japanese Forces Lock and Load with One Eye on China," *Time*, September 23, 2014.

Chinese strategy in the East and South China Seas appears to be far more deliberate than Russia's actions in Ukraine. Although Russia was quick to take advantage of an emerging opportunity and a soft threshold, China has gently probed its way forward, surging only briefly with limited but incrementally effective actions, such as creating the ADIZ. Most recently, China went so far as to build new islands in the Spratly Islands using ships specially designed to dredge and then spray sand; this is one of the more-innovative measures short of war used since 9/11.[22] Experts on Chinese strategy tend to identify three general features to China's approach in the East and South China Seas.

First, China has leveraged economic activity, legal action, trade agreements, and diplomacy to either build space for boundary expansion or establish mutually beneficial relationships with regional and global partners. These mutually beneficial relationships create dependencies that give rivals pause: The U.S. economy is so closely interwoven with the Chinese economy that any military conflict between the two states would probably be catastrophic. Second, China seeks to legitimize its claims by creating the conditions for de facto sovereignty. It takes this strategic approach through a range of measures short of war, some of which Kennan identified and some of which are imaginative and cutting edge. For example, China has used its fishing fleet to establish a recurring presence that contributes to claims of ownership. Third, China creates deterrents to counteraction by establishing its willingness to use limited military force. Chinese strategists appear to have found a relatively safe liminal position between regulated military advance, temporary withdrawal, and overarching threat. Together, these three short-of-war approaches are powerful and very difficult to predict and counter.

This strategy of threshold exploitation and geographic boundary stretching has been largely successful for China at the transactional level. China has redefined the status quo to give legitimacy to its claims, and it has rebuffed counteractions. Neither Japan nor the Philippines has managed to roll back China's increased presence in the disputed areas. However, China has not yet achieved its ostensible objectives, and its aggressive behavior has altered regional behavior in a way that might eventually backfire. Japan remains in administrative control of the Senkaku Islands, and the Philippines is challenging the basis of China's South China Seas claims in a United Nations Convention on the Law of the Sea case. Although the ADIZ remains in place, the U.S. military continues to operate within its boundaries. Moreover, China's assertiveness has caused several regional states—most obviously, Japan and the Philippines—to reinvigorate their own military capabilities and to draw closer to the United States. So if the results thus far have been mixed, why should China's actions be of great concern to U.S. policymakers?

A short-term, tactical view of China's island barrier strategy would lead one to believe that China has been partly successful but has not achieved its objectives. However, if China is enacting a longer-term strategy, it might be edging slowly toward success. RAND researcher Andrew Scobell describes China's deliberate use of measures short of war along these island chains as *slow-intensity conflict*:

> Unlike low intensity conflict, [Chinese] slow intensity conflict entails the possibility of conventional warfighting between the regular armed forces of different states, primarily small units battling in minor and infrequent skirmishes. In addition, slow intensity conflict may

---

[22] See, e.g., Edward Wong and Jonathan Ansfield, "China, Trying to Bolster Its Claims, Plants Islands in Disputed Waters," *New York Times*, June 16, 2014.

involve the use of diplomatic and economic pressure and propaganda. Escalation of such a conflict tends to be slow and incremental, thereby impeding the efforts of any other party to focus international attention on a suspected violation and coordinate a response with neighbors.[23]

In simple terms, then, China is applying a combination of measures short of war to achieve long-term rather than short-term objectives. The mixed tempo of Chinese action has been particularly effective in keeping both regional adversaries and the United States off balance. Although the United States has pushed back against the ADIZ and Japan has pushed back against Chinese civil, police, and military activity, neither the United States nor Japan has displayed a willingness to engage in high-order war over the Senkaku Islands. Barring a major change in Chinese strategy, or the development of an effective and enduring counterstrategy, China appears likely to achieve at least some of its strategic aims in the East and South China Seas.[24]

Example 3: Iran in Iraq

Iran has been a direct competitor of the United States since the fall of Shah Mohammad Reza Pahlavi in 1979. From 1979 through at least late 2011, Iranian politicians, intelligence officers, and proxies made good use of measures short of war to undermine U.S. policy and to kill Americans in the Middle East. Iran supported the Lebanese Hezbollah bombings of the U.S. embassy and the U.S. Marine Corps barracks in Beirut, Lebanon, in 1983 that together killed a total of 258 Americans.[25] According to the Long Commission report on the barracks attack, "Iranian operatives in Lebanon are in the business of killing Americans."[26] Iran was also linked with the bombing of Khobar Towers in Saudi Arabia in 1996, again leveraging Hezbollah proxy agents to kill Americans.[27] It was nothing new, then, for Iran to use the 2003–2011 war in Iraq as an opportunity to oppose U.S. strategy in the Middle East, further its regional interests, and kill U.S. service members and civilians. Iran accomplished all of these objectives expertly and with minimal backlash despite considerable evidence that Iranian weapons and Iranian-trained agents helped to kill or wound well over 100 Americans during the course of the war.

Iran's interests in Iraq are long-standing. The Shi`a theocratic regime has been competing with the United States in Iraq since the onset of the Iran–Iraq war in 1980, just one year after the fall of Pahlavi Shah. The United States provided crucial intelligence support to the Sunni-

---

[23] Andrew Scobell, "Slow-Intensity Conflict in the South China Sea," Philadelphia, Pa.: Foreign Policy Research Institute, August 2000.

[24] Inevitably, some Chinese efforts will fail or deliver only partial success. However, China's long-term approach will give Chinese military and political planners ample time and leeway to make adjustments and additional efforts.

[25] Seventeen Americans were killed at the embassy, and 241 were killed at the barracks.

[26] DoD, *Report of the DoD Commission on Beirut International Airport Terrorist Act, October 23, 1983*, December 20, 1983, p. 61.

[27] See, e.g., National Counterterrorism Center, "Hizballah," *Counterterrorism Guide*, undated; referenced June 5, 2014; and Jonathan Masters and Zachary Laub, "Hezbollah (a.k.a. Hizbollah, Hizbu'llah)," Council on Foreign Relations Backgrounder, January 3, 2014. The Council on Foreign Relations lists Iranian Hezbollah's link to the Khobar Tower attacks as "disputed."

led Saddam Hussein regime from (probably) 1982 through the end of the Iran–Iraq war, help-ing Iraq to temporarily secure control of the strategic Shatt al-Arab waterway.[28] During the same period, Iran facilitated the killing of U.S. citizens in Lebanon and the murder of a U.S. sailor from TWA Flight 847 in 1985.[29] It is not at all clear that these actions were in response to U.S. support for Saddam Hussein, but they did help to solidify the pattern of tit-for-tat use of measures short of war between Iran and the United States. When the U.S.-led coali-tion entered Iraq in 2003, the Iraqi Shi`a majority—with some considerable support from the United States—came to the fore. Iranian leaders saw an opportunity to simultaneously dis-mantle the hated Sunni Iraqi state, to further the interests of the Shi`a Muslim community, and to undermine the United States. Within a year of the invasion, Iran had implemented a multipronged covert-action program in Iraq designed to accomplish all of these objectives.

This covert program, led by the Iranian Revolutionary Guard Corps Quds Force, was an extension of Iran's existing covert-action programs designed to undermine the Saddam Hussein regime.[30] The U.S. invasion of Iraq, and the subsequent chaos and establishment of a strong Shi`a-led government, allowed the Quds Force to accelerate its efforts. In 2008, then–U.S. Ambassador Ryan Crocker stated that Iran was fighting a proxy war in Iraq against the United States.[31] Over the course of the war, Iran provided hundreds of explosively formed penetrator devices, RPG-29 antitank rockets, and both 107-mm and 240-mm rockets, among other resources. These weapons probably killed and wounded hundreds, if not thousands, of Americans.[32] The Quds Force leveraged its most effective proxy force, Lebanese Hezbollah, to help coordinate and implement its covert actions in Iraq, including attacks against Americans. In 2007, U.S. BG Kevin Bergner, then senior director for Iraq on the NSC staff, and the *New York Times* described the Iranian-backed use of Lebanese Hezbollah in Iraq, just after the cap-ture of senior Lebanese Hezbollah leader Ali Moussa Dakdouk in southern Iraq:[33]

> Dakdouk is accused of being a 24-year veteran of Hezbollah, and was "tasked to orga-nize the special groups in ways that mirrored how Hezbollah was organized in Lebanon," Bergner said. . . . Hezbollah, Bergner said, helped the Iranians "to do things they didn't want to have to do themselves in terms of interacting with special groups." . . . Dakdouk was captured with documents instructing the special groups on techniques, including how to attack a convoy, and with a personal diary detailing meetings with Iraqi militants. . . .

---

[28] See, e.g., Seymour M. Hersh, "U.S. Secretly Gave Aid to Iraq Early in Its War Against Iran," *New York Times*, Janu-ary 26, 1992.

[29] See, e.g., William E. Smith, "Terror Aboard Flight 847," *Time*, June 24, 2001.

[30] Joseph H. Felter and Brian Fishman, *Iranian Strategy in Iraq: Politics and "Other Means,"* West Point, N.Y.: Combat-ting Terrorism Center, U.S. Military Academy, October 13, 2008, pp. 21–24. That paper was derived primarily from U.S. government Harmony database documents that provide direct insight into Iranian covert activities and intentions. Also see Kimberly Kagan, "Iran's Proxy War Against the United States and the Iraqi Government," *Iraq Report, May 2006–August 20, 2007*, pp. 1–32.

[31] Helene Cooper, "Iran Fighting Proxy War in Iraq, U.S. Envoy Says," *New York Times*, April 12, 2008.

[32] See, e.g., see James Glanz, "U.S. Says Arms Link to Iranian Shiites," *New York Times*, February 12, 2007; Kagan, 2007; Sameer N. Yacoub, "US Says Iran Smuggling Missiles to Iraq," *Washington Post*, September 24, 2007; and Michael Knights, "Iran's Ongoing Proxy War in Iraq," Washington, D.C.: Washington Institute for Near East Policy, Policywatch 1492, March 16, 2009.

[33] "U.S. Accuses Hezbollah of Aiding Iran in Iraq," *New York Times*, July 2, 2007.

[Another Lebanese Hezbollah operative] Khazaali [was captured with] documents with details on 11 separate attacks on U.S. forces, the general said.

And as Joseph Felter and Brian Fishman point out in their report on Iranian strategy in Iraq, Iran made extensive use of economic, political, religious, and diplomatic measures that coincided neatly with the Quds Force covert-action plan.[34] All Iranian measures short of high-order war were on the table from 2003 through 2011, including the investment of possibly hundreds of millions of dollars in Iraqi infrastructure, similar amounts in direct and indirect humanitarian aid, political and religious coercion, and many of the other measures that Kennan described. Although some Iranian efforts were uncovered, many others probably went unnoticed, and the United States was never able to stop Iran from implementing its plans.

Whether or not the Iranian strategy in Iraq from 2003 to 2011 was carefully planned, like the Chinese strategy in the East and South China Seas, or more opportunistic, like the Russian strategy in Ukraine in 2014–2015, Iranian success has been remarkable. During the first 23 years after the onset of the Iran–Iraq war in 1980, Iran made little headway against the Iraqi state. After the U.S.-led invasion in 2003, Iran greatly accelerated its activities and began to reap much greater rewards. Iran succeeded in Iraq using measures short of war honed in the 1980s and 1990s. Although U.S. military officers and policymakers complained about Iranian involvement in Iraq and about Iran's direct involvement in the killing of Americans, there were few repercussions for Iranian actions. The United States maintains sanctions against Iran to address its nuclear program, but it took no overt actions to punish Iran for the Quds Force covert action in Iraq. Essentially, therefore, Iran managed to actively kill and wound perhaps hundreds of Americans and severely undermine a major U.S. military campaign without significant strategic consequence. Arguably, this is threshold exploitation and stretching of the first order. As of mid-2015, Iran appeared to have greater influence over the government of Iraq than any other country had; it had overtly deployed Quds Force battalions into northeastern Iraq, and it was conducting airstrikes on Iraqi territory in support of Iraqi ground forces. Greatly as a result of Iran's successful use of measures short of war, Iraq might yet become an Iranian proxy state, and the United States has lost much influence over a critical Middle Eastern ally.

---

[34] Felter and Fishman, 2008. The authors wove examples throughout their report.

CHAPTER FOUR

Conclusion, Considerations, and Cautions

Threshold exploitation and threshold stretching are, for nation-states, time-tested and practically reflexive actions; this is nothing new. Russia, China, and Iran have simply been practicing "old-school" cutthroat international relations: They have expertly used measures short of war to expand their influence and create time and space for future action while carefully managing the risk of U.S. response. Each country has either identified and exploited a soft spot in U.S. policy and willpower or, viewed through a different lens of analysis, taken advantage of the gray areas inherent in tacit regional thresholds for high-order war. Each country has leveraged new technology and sophisticated, mutually supporting political, economic, diplomatic, legal, intelligence, and military tactics to gain advantage. And each country has, to varying degrees and perhaps as a second- rather than first-order purpose, eroded U.S. regional influence, as well as the implicit power of America's deterrent military force. This disquieting post–Iraq and Afghanistan trend is redolent of the post–Vietnam War era, during which the Soviet Union made efforts to capitalize on U.S. malaise to undermine its deterrence and influence. U.S. policymakers and military service leaders should be concerned with the regional problems in Ukraine, the East and South China Seas, and the Middle East, but they should perhaps be more concerned with the broader problem of strategic vulnerability.

Nothing can be done to *eliminate* the threat that measures short of war pose. As Rupert Smith and most realists convincingly argue, states are always in conflict at some level. George Kennan also proposed this paradigm of continuous conflict and shrugs aside the notion of fixed thresholds between war and nonwar. He suggests that the best way to address this reality is to develop and maintain an effective U.S. grand strategy that seamlessly incorporates measures short of war into a long-term, globally integrated plan:[1]

> We must select measures and use them not hit-or-miss as the moment may seem to demand, but in accordance with a pattern of grand strategy no less concrete and no less consistent than that which governs our actions in war. It is my own conviction that we must go even further than that and must cease to have separate patterns of measures—one pattern for peace and one pattern for war. Rather, we must select them according to the purpose we are pursuing and classify them that way. We must work out a general plan of what the U.S. wants in this world and pursue that plan with all the measures at our disposal, depending on what is indicated by the circumstances.

Yet a great deal can be done to blunt or reverse the impact of competitors' use of measures short of war. Unfortunately, the United States has not and probably will not be a nation that

---

[1] Kennan, 1991, pp. 16–17.

can develop and maintain a comprehensive, long-term global strategy in the post–Cold War era. Increasingly partisan national elections all but ensure major shifts in strategic outlook over relatively short periods of time. U.S. strategic culture is not predisposed to fixed planning at the level above what are now termed combatant commands (e.g., U.S. Central Command). Because U.S. leaders tend to envision global interests and responsibilities, the challenge of developing an integrated strategy is exponentially more complex than for nations interested mostly in immediate national and regional issues. These are disadvantages in that the United States is often unprepared to deal with emerging crises. Further, the United States cannot be perfectly ready to counter any and all conceivable political, economic, legal, intelligence, or military threats around the world. There will never be sufficient political will or resources to promote or even defend U.S. interests in every situation and location. Periodic retrenchment is part and parcel of international relations.

Despite these enduring challenges, U.S. policymakers should still consider ways to reduce U.S. strategic vulnerabilities and to develop a more-robust capability to rapidly counter and exploit events like the Russian seizure of Crimea. Although the United States struggles to fit the use of measures short of war into its global and regional planning, there are many examples of situations in which the United States has succeeded in using measures short of war at what might be called the "tactical" level. Many covert actions by the Central Intelligence Agency (CIA) have succeeded, and the most successful of these will probably remain hidden to the public. U.S. aid to foreign military forces since the beginning of the Cold War has led to a muddied record of successes and failures, but such actions as foreign internal defense and unconventional warfare continue to offer attractive options for policymakers. The value of these approaches is now emerging in more-aggressive and better-funded theater security cooperation plans at each U.S. combatant command. And as the United States demonstrated in response to the Russian invasion of Crimea, the more-overt measures short of war, such as economic sanctions, can have real impact.

Considerations

All of the possible capabilities and actions that constitute measures short of war should be considered and, where feasible, developed or sharpened. Although U.S. capabilities to rebuff threshold stretching and exploitation will never be perfect, they can be considerably improved to provide policymakers with both new capabilities and well-developed concepts and regionally aligned threshold defense and exploitation plans. Although the scope of this research project did not include the development of specific recommendations, we offer several broad considerations for policymakers:

- *Response tools and response tempo must be improved.* Examples of insufficient or inadequately paced responses to threshold exploitation and stretching attacks on U.S. interests demonstrate a clear need for more-effective military, clandestine, diplomatic, economic, and communication *response* measures. These measures should be designed for rapid implementation in order to offset strategic surprise.
- *U.S. national security organizations must provide holistic, well-informed options.* In order to prevent or respond to threshold exploitation and stretching short of high-order war, U.S. national security organizations must present the President with policy options, strategic

choices, and response options. This would require holistic analysis of the problem in both regional and global contexts, including recommendations for strategic objectives, risks, and potential gains from a possible range of mutually reinforcing actions or nonactions.

- *Improved strategic response demands improved expertise in the use of measures short of war.* Elements of the U.S. government responsible for advising the President on policies, strategies, and response options need to develop in-house expertise specifically tailored to provide holistic, mutually supporting measures short of war.
- *Specific military capabilities should flow from strategic requirements for measures short of war.* In many cases, these capabilities already exist (e.g., foreign internal defense, demonstrations of force, and military information support operations). Other capabilities will have to be repurposed or developed.

Doing these things well would require a level of focus and attention that, as events in Crimea, the East and South China Seas, and Iraq have shown, has not been clearly articulated and acted upon. Recent efforts by the U.S. Special Operations Command and other combatant and component commands and military services to focus on "Phase Zero" show that DoD is already focusing on what might be termed "prewar" capabilities and deterrents. These can be expanded or modified into more-active offensive and defensive tools for threshold reinforcement or for U.S. actions to exploit and stretch regional thresholds. The national security research community can and should support DoD and the services in better understanding the opportunities, risks, and costs of the military aspects of these requirements.

The Risks of Improving and Increasing the Use of Measures Short of War

Risk assessment and an understanding of reasonable limitations should be integral to any effort to improve U.S. measures short of war. Although the CIA has had many notable successes in the late 20th and early 21st centuries, during the late 1960s and early 1970s, it allowed its operations directorate to use measures short of war in a way that was, arguably, counterproductive to U.S. international interests.[2] And although foreign internal defense and unconventional warfare—two of the most prominent military measures short of war—have proven useful, engaging everywhere at all times around the world also exposes the United States to additional risk and costs. Improving measures-short-of-war capabilities and reducing risks to negotiated and tacit thresholds will require careful balancing between improvement in tactical capability and risks to U.S. prestige, influence, treasury, and moral standing.

---

[2] The Church Committee (U.S. Senate Select Committee to Study Governmental Operations with Respect to Intelligence Activities), Rockefeller Commission (U.S. President's Commission on CIA Activities Within the United States), and Pike Committee (U.S. House Permanent Select Committee on Intelligence), as well as critical assessments by members of the intelligence community in the past several decades, have documented these excesses. See U.S. Commission on CIA Activities Within the United States, *Report to the President*, Washington, D.C.: U.S. Government Printing Office, 1975; Timothy S. Hardy, "Intelligence Reform in the Mid-1970s," *Studies Archive Indexes*, Vol. 20, No. 2, February 23, 2010; Gerald K. Haines, "The Pike Committee Investigations and the CIA: Looking for a Rogue Elephant," *Studies in Intelligence*, Winter 1998–1999; and L. Britt Snider, "Recollections from the Church Committee's Investigation of NSA: Unlucky SHAMROCK," *Studies in Intelligence*, Winter 1999–2000.

Bibliography

Achen, Christopher H., and Duncan Snidal, "Rational Deterrence Theory and Comparative Case Studies," *World Politics*, Vol. 41, No. 2, January 1989, pp. 143–169.

Allison, Graham T., and Philip Zelikow, *Essence of Decision: Explaining the Cuban Missile Crisis*, 2nd ed., New York: Longman, 1999.

Applebaum, Anne, "Putin's New Kind of War," *Slate*, April 16, 2014. As of June 9, 2014:
http://www.slate.com/articles/news_and_politics/foreigners/2014/04/
vladimir_putin_s_new_war_in_ukraine_the_kremlin_is_reinventing_how_russia.html

Bader, Jeffrey A., "The U.S. and China's Nine-Dash Line: Ending the Ambiguity," Washington, D.C.: Brookings Institution, February 6, 2014. As of April 23, 2015:
http://www.brookings.edu/research/opinions/2014/02/06-us-china-nine-dash-line-bader

Bassford, Christopher, *Clausewitz and His Works*, March 18, 2013. As of May 6, 2014:
http://www.clausewitz.com/readings/Bassford/Cworks/Works.htm

Beckley, Michael, "China's Century? Why America's Edge Will Endure," *International Security*, Vol. 36, No. 3, Winter 2011–2012, pp. 41–78. As of April 23, 2015:
http://belfercenter.ksg.harvard.edu/publication/21649/chinas_century_why_americas_edge_will_endure.html

Betts, Richard K., "Surprise Despite Warning: Why Sudden Attacks Succeed," *Political Science Quarterly*, Vol. 95, No. 4, Winter 1980–1981, pp. 551–572.

"Bill Clinton: We Could Have Saved 3,000 Lives in Rwanda," CNBC, March 13, 2013. As of May 5, 2015:
http://www.cnbc.com/id/100546207

Black, C. E., "Diplomatic History: The Soviet Approach—A Review Article," *American Slavic and East European Review*, Vol. 7, No. 3, October 1948, pp. 276–288.

Blank, Stephen, "The Chinese Concept of 'Unrestricted Warfare': Global Competitors Up the Ante," *Second Line of Defense*, April 11, 2014. As of May 5, 2014:
http://www.sldinfo.com/the-chinese-concept-of-unrestricted-warfare-global-competitors-up-the-ante/

Blumenthal, Daniel, "Riding a Tiger: China's Resurging Foreign Policy Aggression," *Foreign Policy*, April 15, 2011. As of April 23, 2015:
http://foreignpolicy.com/2011/04/15/riding-a-tiger-chinas-resurging-foreign-policy-aggression/

Bohlen, Celestine, "Cold War Media Tactics Fuel Ukraine Crisis," *New York Times*, March 10, 2014. As of April 23, 2015:
http://www.nytimes.com/2014/03/11/world/europe/cold-war-media-tactics-fuel-ukraine-crisis.html

Bouchat, Clarence J., *Dangerous Ground: The Spratly Islands and U.S. Interests and Approaches*, Carlisle Barracks, Pa.: U.S. Army War College Press, December 27, 2013. As of April 23, 2015:
http://www.strategicstudiesinstitute.army.mil/pubs/display.cfm?pubID=1187

Brandt, Willy, "The Means Short of War," *Foreign Affairs*, January 1961. As of April 9, 2014:
http://www.foreignaffairs.com/articles/71598/willy-brandt/the-means-short-of-war

Bremer, Stuart A., "Dangerous Dyads: Conditions Affecting the Likelihood of Interstate War, 1816–1965," *Journal of Conflict Resolution*, Vol. 36, No. 2, June 1992, pp. 309–341.

Brown, Michael E., Owen R. Coté, Sean M. Lynn-Jones, and Steven E. Miller, eds., *Rational Choice and Security Studies: Stephen Walt and His Critics*, Cambridge, Mass.: MIT Press, 2000.

Brzezinski, Zbigniew, "Middle East," Washington, D.C.: White House, Presidential Review Memorandum/National Security Council Paper 3, January 21, 1977. As of April 23, 2015:
http://fas.org/irp/offdocs/prm/prm03.pdf

Bueno de Mesquita, Bruce, "The Costs of War: A Rational Expectations Approach," *American Political Science Review*, Vol. 77, No. 2, June 1983, pp. 347–357.

———, "Toward a Scientific Understanding of International Conflict: A Personal View," *International Studies Quarterly*, Vol. 29, No. 2, June 1985, pp. 121–136.

Bueno de Mesquita, Bruce, and David Lalman, *War and Reason: Domestic and International Imperatives*, New Haven, Conn.: Yale University Press, 1992.

Bueno de Mesquita, Bruce, and James D. Morrow, "Sorting Through the Wealth of Notions," *International Security*, Vol. 24, No. 2, Fall 1999, pp. 56–73.

Bueno De Mesquita, Bruce, James D. Morrow, Randolph M. Siverson, and Alastair Smith, "An Institutional Explanation of the Democratic Peace," *American Political Science Review*, Vol. 93, No. 4, December 1999, pp. 791–807.

Bundy, McGeorge, untitled memorandum for the Secretary of State, the Secretary of Defense, and the Director of Central Intelligence, Washington, D.C.: White House, National Security Action Memorandum 328, April 6, 1965a. As of January 1, 2015:
http://www.lbjlib.utexas.edu/johnson/archives.hom/NSAMs/nsam328.asp

———, "Preparation of Arms Control Program," Washington, D.C.: White House, National Security Action Memorandum 335, June 28, 1965b. As of January 1, 2015:
http://www.lbjlib.utexas.edu/johnson/archives.hom/NSAMs/nsam335.asp

Bush, George H. W., *National Security Strategy of the United States*, Washington, D.C.: White House, August 1, 1991. As of April 23, 2015:
http://nssarchive.us/national-security-strategy-1991/

Bush, George W., *National Security Strategy of the United States of America*, Washington, D.C.: White House, March 2006. As of April 23, 2015:
http://nssarchive.us/national-security-strategy-2006/

Carter, Jimmy, "U.S. National Strategy," Washington, D.C.: White House, Presidential Directive/National Security Council Paper 18, August 26, 1977a. As of April 23, 2015:
https://fas.org/irp/offdocs/pd/pd18.pdf

———, "Policy Toward Eastern Europe," Washington, D.C.: White House, Presidential Directive/National Security Council Paper 21, September 13, 1977b. As of April 23, 2015:
https://fas.org/irp/offdocs/pd/pd21.pdf

Chatterjee, Partha, "On the Rational Choice Theory of Limited Strategic War," *Indian Journal of Political Science*, Vol. 34, No. 2, April–June 1973, pp. 157–172.

Chen, Dingding, Xiaoyu Pu, and Alastair Iain Johnston, "Correspondence: Debating China's Assertiveness," *International Security*, Vol. 38, No. 3, Winter 2013–2014.

Christopher, Warren, "PRM on Human Rights," Washington, D.C.: Office of the Deputy Secretary of State, Presidential Review Memorandum/National Security Council Paper 28, July 8, 1977. As of April 23, 2015:
http://fas.org/irp/offdocs/prm/prm28.pdf

Clinton, Bill, *A National Security Strategy of Engagement and Enlargement*, Washington, D.C.: White House, July 1, 1994. As of April 23, 2015:
http://nssarchive.us/national-security-strategy-1994/

———, *A National Security Strategy for a New Century*, Washington, D.C.: White House, 1998. As of May 11, 2015:
http://nssarchive.us/national-security-strategy-1998/

Cooper, Helene, "Iran Fighting Proxy War in Iraq, U.S. Envoy Says," *New York Times*, April 12, 2008. As of June 9, 2014:
http://www.nytimes.com/2008/04/12/world/middleeast/12policy.html

Craig, Gordon Alexander, and Alexander L. George, *Force and Statecraft: Diplomatic Problems of Our Time*, 3rd ed., New York: Oxford University Press, 1995.

Davis, Jeanne W., "Minutes of NSC Meeting Held December 15, 1976," memorandum for Brent Scowcroft, Washington, D.C.: National Security Council, January 3, 1977. As of January 1, 2015:
http://www.fordlibrarymuseum.gov/library/document/0312/1552410.pdf

Davis, Paul K., and Peter A. Wilson, *Looming Discontinuities in U.S. Military Strategy and Defense Planning: Colliding RMAs Necessitate a New Strategy*, Santa Monica, Calif.: RAND Corporation, OP-326-OSD, 2011. As of April 23, 2015:
http://www.rand.org/pubs/occasional_papers/OP326.html

"Declassified Government Reports to Document USSR Personnel in VN," undated archive summary, Texas Tech University Vietnam Online Archives.

Denyer, Simon, "China Bypasses American 'New Silk Road' with Two If [sic] Its Own," *Washington Post*, October 14, 2013. As of April 23, 2015:
http://www.washingtonpost.com/world/asia_pacific/
china-bypasses-american-new-silk-road-with-two-if-its-own/2013/10/14/
49f9f60c-3284-11e3-ad00-ec4c6b31cbed_story.html

Denyer, Simon, and Chico Harlan, "China Sends Warplanes to Patrol New Air Defense Zone," *Washington Post*, November 29, 2013. As of April 23, 2015:
http://www.washingtonpost.com/world/china-sends-warplanes-to-patrol-new-air-defense-zone/2013/11/28/
a723bfdc-5874-11e3-bdbf-097ab2a3dc2b_story.html

De Waal, Tom, "Soft Annexation of Abkhazia Is the Greatest Legacy of Putin to His Successor," interview by Alexander Jackson, *Caucasian Review of International Affairs*, Vol. 2, No. 3, Summer 2008, pp. 173–177. As of April 24, 2015:
http://www.cria-online.org/4_7.html

Dinstein, Yoram, "The Legal Issues of 'Para-War' and Peace in the Middle East," *St. John's Law Review*, Vol. 44, No. 3, January 1970, pp. 466–482.

Dobbins, James, David C. Gompert, David A. Shlapak, and Andrew Scobell, *Conflict with China: Prospects, Consequences, and Strategies for Deterrence*, Santa Monica, Calif.: RAND Corporation, OP-344-A, 2011. As of April 23, 2015:
http://www.rand.org/pubs/occasional_papers/OP344.html

DoD—*See* U.S. Department of Defense.

Donnelly, Jack, *Realism and International Relations*, Cambridge, UK: Cambridge University Press, 2000.

Drezner, Daniel W., "Bad Debts: Assessing China's Financial Influence in Great Power Politics," *International Security*, Vol. 34, No. 2, Fall 2009, pp. 7–45.

Elder, Miriam, "CEO of 'Russian Facebook' Says He Was Fired and That the Social Network Is Now in the Hands of Putin Allies," *Buzzfeed News*, April 21, 2014. As of April 24, 2015:
http://www.buzzfeed.com/miriamelder/ceo-of-russian-facebook-says-he-was-fired-and-that-the-socia

Fearon, James D., "Rationalist Explanations for War," *International Organization*, Vol. 49, No. 3, Summer 1995, pp. 379–414.

Fearon, James D., and David D. Laitin, "Ethnicity, Insurgency, and Civil War," *American Political Science Review*, Vol. 97, No. 1, February 2003, pp. 75–90.

Felter, Joseph H., and Brian Fishman, *Iranian Strategy in Iraq: Politics and "Other Means,"* West Point, N.Y.: Combatting Terrorism Center, U.S. Military Academy, October 13, 2008.

Forsyth, Michael, "Finesse: A Theory Short of War," *Military Review*, July–August 2004, pp. 17–19. As of April 7, 2014:
http://www.au.af.mil/au/awc/awcgate/milreview/forsyth.pdf

Fravel, M. Taylor, "Power Shifts and Escalation: Explaining China's Use of Force in Territorial Disputes," *International Security*, Vol. 32, No. 3, Winter 2007–2008, pp. 44–83.

Fravel, M. Taylor, and Evan Medeiros, "China's Search for Assured Retaliation: The Evolution of Chinese Nuclear Strategy and Force Structure," *International Security*, Vol. 35, No. 2, Fall 2010, pp. 48–87.

Fuller, L. N., "British Steamer Is Burned by the Patriots," in *Northern New York in the Patriot War*, Watertown, N.Y.: Brockway Company, 1923.

Gavin, Francis J., "The Myth of Flexible Response: United States Strategy in Europe During the 1960s," *International History Review*, Vol. 23, No. 4, December 2001, pp. 847–875.

George, Alexander L., "The 'Operational Code': A Neglected Approach to the Study of Political Leaders and Decision-Making," *International Studies Quarterly*, Vol. 13, No. 2, June 1969, pp. 190–222.

George, Alexander L., and William E. Simons, eds. *The Limits of Coercive Diplomacy*, Boulder, Colo.: Westview Press, 1994.

Glanz, James, "U.S. Says Arms Link to Iranian Shiites," *New York Times*, February 12, 2007. As of June 5, 2014:
http://www.nytimes.com/2007/02/12/world/middleeast/12weapons.html

Goldgeier, James "Stop Blaming NATO for Putin's Provocations," *New Republic*, April 17, 2014. As of April 24, 2015:
http://www.newrepublic.com/article/117423/nato-not-blame-putins-actions

Goldstone, Jack A., "Bad to Worse in Ukraine?" *NewPopulationBomb*, April 11, 2014. As of April 24, 2015:
http://newpopulationbomb.com/2014/04/11/bad-to-worse-in-ukraine/

Gordon, Michael R., and Andrew E. Kramer, "Scrutiny over Photos Said to Tie Russia Units to Ukraine," *New York Times*, April 22, 2014. As of May 7, 2014:
http://www.nytimes.com/2014/04/23/world/europe/
scrutiny-over-photos-said-to-tie-russia-units-to-ukraine.html

Gray, Colin S., "National Style in Strategy: The American Example," *International Security*, Vol. 6, No. 2, Fall 1981, pp. 21–47.

Haddick, Robert, "The Civilianization of War," *National Interest*, April 11, 2014. As of April 24, 2015:
http://nationalinterest.org/commentary/the-civilianization-war-10229

Hadley, Stephen J., and Damon Wilson, "Putin's Takeover of Crimea Is Part of a Larger Strategy," *Washington Post*, March 3, 2014. As of April 24, 2015:
http://www.washingtonpost.com/opinions/putins-takeover-of-crimea-is-part-of-a-larger-strategy/2014/03/03/a9cd5d7a-a2ec-11e3-84d4-e59b1709222c_story.html

Haines, Gerald K., "The Pike Committee Investigations and the CIA: Looking for a Rogue Elephant," *Studies in Intelligence*, Winter 1998–1999. As of January 3, 2015:
https://www.cia.gov/library/center-for-the-study-of-intelligence/csi-publications/csi-studies/studies/winter98_99/art07.html

Halperin, Morton H., *Limited War in the Nuclear Age*, New York: Wiley, 1963.

Hardy, Timothy S., "Intelligence Reform in the Mid-1970s," *Studies Archive Indexes*, Vol. 20, No. 2, February 23, 2010. As of January 3, 2015:
https://www.cia.gov/library/center-for-the-study-of-intelligence/kent-csi/vol20no2/html/v20i2a01p_0001.htm

Harlow, Bryce, and Dave Gergen, "National Security Speech," drafts of speech and memorandum of transmittal to Dick Cheney, Washington, D.C.: White House, March 28, 1976. As of January 1, 2015:
http://www.fordlibrarymuseum.gov/library/document/0067/1563080.pdf

Heeg, Jason, *Chinese Imperialism in 2013: Application of Unrestricted Warfare or the Legitimate Use of the Economic Instrument of National Power?* Fort Leavenworth, Kan.: Foreign Military Studies Office, September 29, 2013. As of May 5, 2014:
http://fmso.leavenworth.army.mil/collaboration/interagency/chinese-imperialism.pdf

Hersh, Seymour M., "U.S. Secretly Gave Aid to Iraq Early in Its War Against Iran," *New York Times*, January 26, 1992. As of June 9, 2014:
http://www.nytimes.com/1992/01/26/world/us-secretly-gave-aid-to-iraq-early-in-its-war-against-iran.html

Hill, Fiona, and Steven Pifer, "Putin's Russia Goes Rogue," in Ted Piccone, Steven Pifer, and Thomas Wright, eds., *Big Bets and Black Swans: A Presidential Briefing Book*, Brookings Institution, January 2014, pp. 35–37. As of April 24, 2015:
http://www.brookings.edu/research/papers/2014/01/putin-russia-rogue-hill-pifer

Hoffman, Frank G., "Hybrid Warfare and Challenges," *Joint Forces Quarterly*, No. 52, first quarter 2009. As of April 24, 2015:
http://smallwarsjournal.com/documents/jfqhoffman.pdf

Huth, Paul, and Bruce Russett, "Deterrence Failure and Crisis Escalation," *International Studies Quarterly*, Vol. 32, No. 1, March 1988, pp. 29–45.

Jervis, Robert, *Perception and Misperception in International Politics*, Princeton, N.J.: Princeton University Press, 1976.

———, "Political Implications of Loss Aversion," *Political Psychology*, Vol. 13, No. 2, June 1992, pp. 187–204.

Johns Hopkins University Applied Physics Laboratory, "2009 Unrestricted Warfare Symposium," c. 2009. As of May 5, 2014:
http://www.jhuapl.edu/urw_symposium/

Johnston, Alastair Iain, *Cultural Realism: Strategic Culture and Grand Strategy in Chinese History*, Princeton, N.J.: Princeton University Press, 1995a.

———, "Thinking About Strategic Culture," *International Security*, Vol. 19, No. 4, Spring 1995b, pp. 32–64.

Kagan, Kimberly, "Iran's Proxy War Against the United States and the Iraqi Government," *Iraq Report*, May 2006–August 20, 2007, pp. 1–32. As of June 5, 2014:
https://www.understandingwar.org/sites/default/files/reports/IraqReport06.pdf

Kahn, Herman, *On Thermonuclear War*, Princeton, N.J.: Princeton University Press, 1960.

———, *On Escalation: Metaphors and Scenarios*, New York: Praeger, 1965.

Kaplan, Fred, "Why Putin May Stand Down," *Slate*, April 14, 2014. As of April 24, 2015:
http://www.slate.com/articles/news_and_politics/war_stories/2014/04/
vladimir_putin_may_not_invade_ukraine_can_russia_s_president_succeed_without.html

Keating, Kenneth C., Maskirovka: *The Soviet System of Camouflage*, Garmisch, Germany: U.S. Army Russian Institute, 1981. As of May 11, 2015:
http://www.dtic.mil/dtic/tr/fulltext/u2/a112903.pdf

Kennan, George F., "Inauguration of Organized Political Warfare," Washington, D.C.: *Foreign Relations of the United States, 1945–1950*, Retrospective Volume, *Emergence of the Intelligence Establishment*, Policy Planning Staff Memorandum, Document 269, May 4, 1948. As of April 14, 2014:
http://history.state.gov/historicaldocuments/frus1945-50Intel/d269

———, in Giles D. Harlow and George C. Maerz, eds., *Measures Short of War: The George F. Kennan Lectures at the National War College, 1946–1947*, Washington, D.C.: National Defense University Press, 1991.

Khalidi, Ahmed S., "The War of Attrition," *Journal of Palestine Studies*, Vol. 3, No. 1, Autumn 1973, pp. 60–87.

Kissinger, Henry A., *The Necessity for Choice: Prospects of American Foreign Policy*, New York: Harper, 1961.

———, "Criteria for Strategic Sufficiency," Washington, D.C.: National Security Council, National Security Decision Memorandum 16, June 24, 1969. As of April 24, 2015:
http://fas.org/irp/offdocs/nsdm-nixon/nsdm-16.pdf

———, "U.S. Policy Toward the Persian Gulf," Washington, D.C.: National Security Council, National Security Decision Memorandum 92, November 7, 1970. As of April 24, 2015:
http://fas.org/irp/offdocs/nsdm-nixon/nsdm-92.pdf

Knights, Michael, "Iran's Ongoing Proxy War in Iraq," Washington, D.C.: Washington Institute for Near East Policy, Policywatch 1492, March 16, 2009. As of June 5, 2014:
http://www.washingtoninstitute.org/policy-analysis/view/irans-ongoing-proxy-war-in-iraq

———, "The Evolution of Iran's Special Groups in Iraq," *CTC Sentinel*, Vol. 3, No. 11–12, November 2010, pp. 12–16. As of May 27, 2014:
http://www.washingtoninstitute.org/uploads/Documents/opeds/4d06325a6031b.pdf

Kulick, Jonathan, and Paul K. Davis, *Modeling Adversaries and Related Cognitive Biases*, Santa Monica, Calif.: RAND Corporation, RP-1084, 2003. As of April 24, 2015:
http://www.rand.org/pubs/reprints/RP1084.html

Lamothe, Dan, "Marines to Extend Georgia Training Mission," *Marine Corps Times*, April 6, 2011. As of May 7, 2014:
http://www.marinecorpstimes.com/article/20110406/NEWS/104060330/Marines-extend-Georgia-training-mission

Lay, James S., Jr., *A Report to the National Security Council*, Washington, D.C.: National Security Council Paper 68, April 14, 1950. As of December 31, 2014:
https://www.trumanlibrary.org/whistlestop/study_collections/coldwar/documents/pdf/10-1.pdf

Layton, Robert, "The Effect of Measures Short of War on Treaties," *University of Chicago Law Review*, Vol. 30, No. 1, Autumn 1962, pp. 96–119.

Legge, J. Michael, *Theater Nuclear Weapons and the NATO Strategy of Flexible Response*, Santa Monica, Calif.: RAND Corporation, R-2964-FF, 1983. As of April 24, 2015:
http://www.rand.org/pubs/reports/R2964.html

Legro, Jeffrey W., and Andrew Moravcsik, "Is Anybody Still a Realist?" *International Security*, Vol. 24, No. 2, Fall 1999, pp. 5–55.

Levy, Jack S., "Prospect Theory, Rational Choice, and International Relations," *International Studies Quarterly*, Vol. 41, No. 1, March 1997, pp. 87–112.

Londoño, Ernesto, "Ahead of Beijing Visit, Defense Secretary Hagel Admonishes China," *Washington Post*, April 6, 2014. As of May 11, 2015:
http://www.washingtonpost.com/world/us-defense-secretary-hagel-promises-tough-love-for-china-on-eve-of-visit/2014/04/06/f7ae7672-8f67-4291-aee0-64c4d26790de_story.html

Luman, Ronald R., ed., *Unrestricted Warfare Symposium 2009: Proceedings on Combating the Unrestricted Warfare Threat—Terrorism, Resources, Economics, and Cyberspace*, Laurel, Md.: Johns Hopkins University Applied Physics Laboratory, 2009. As of April 24, 2015:
http://www.jhuapl.edu/urw_symposium/Proceedings/2009/Book/2009URWBook.pdf

MacCoby, Simon, "Reprisals as a Measure of Redress Short of War," *Cambridge Law Journal*, Vol. 2, No. 1, 1924, pp. 60–73.

Mankoff, Jeffrey, "Russia's Latest Land Grab: How Putin Won Crimea and Lost Ukraine," *Foreign Affairs*, May–June 2014. As of April 24, 2015:
http://www.foreignaffairs.com/articles/141210/jeffrey-mankoff/russias-latest-land-grab

Marson, James, "Protesters in Ukraine's Restive East Feel Far from Kiev, Close to Russia," *Wall Street Journal*, April 14, 2014. As of April 24, 2015:
http://www.wsj.com/articles/SB10001424052702303887804579501841849966968

Masters, Jonathan, and Zachary Laub, "Hezbollah (a.k.a. Hizbollah, Hizbu'llah)," Council on Foreign Relations Backgrounder, January 3, 2014. As of June 5, 2014:
http://www.cfr.org/lebanon/hezbollah-k-hizbollah-hizbullah/p9155

McMaster, H. R., *Battle of 73 Easting*, U.S. Army, undated. As of May 6, 2014:
http://www.benning.army.mil/Library/content/McMasterHR%20CPT_Battleof73Easting.pdf

Metz, Steven, "In Ukraine, Russia Reveals Its Mastery of Unrestricted Warfare," *World Politics Review*, April 16, 2014. As of April 24, 2015:
http://www.worldpoliticsreview.com/articles/13708/
in-ukraine-russia-reveals-its-mastery-of-unrestricted-warfare

Metz, Steven, and James Kievit, *The Revolution in Military Affairs and Conflict Short of War*, Carlisle Barracks, Pa.: Strategic Studies Institute, U.S. Army War College, July 25, 1994. As of April 9, 2014:
http://www.strategicstudiesinstitute.army.mil/pdffiles/pub241.pdf

Miller, Hunter, ed., "The *Caroline*," *Treaties and Other International Acts of the United States of America*, Vol. 4, Documents 80–121, Washington, D.C.: Government Printing Office, 1934, pp. 1836–1846. As of May 5, 2014:
http://avalon.law.yale.edu/19th_century/br-1842d.asp

Miller, James E., "Taking Off the Gloves: The United States and the Italian Elections of 1948," *Diplomatic History*, Vol. 7, No. 1, January 1983, pp. 35–56.

Mitchell, Gordon R., and Robert P. Newman, "By 'Any Measures' Necessary: NSC-68 and Cold War Roots of the 2002 National Security Strategy," Pittsburgh, Pa.: University of Pittsburgh Department of Communications, 2006. As of April 27, 2015:
https://www.gspia.pitt.edu/Portals/1/pdfs/Publications/MitchellNewman.pdf

Morgan, Forrest E., Karl P. Mueller, Evan S. Medeiros, Kevin L. Pollpeter, and Roger Cliff, *Dangerous Thresholds: Managing Escalation in the 21st Century*, Santa Monica, Calif.: RAND Corporation, MG-614-AF, 2008. As of April 27, 2015:
http://www.rand.org/pubs/monographs/MG614.html

Morgan, Patrick M., *Deterrence: A Conceptual Analysis*, Beverly Hills, Calif.: Sage Publications, 1977.

Morgenthau, Hans J., *Politics Among Nations: The Struggle for Power and Peace*, New York: A. A. Knopf, 1948.

———, "The Four Paradoxes of Nuclear Strategy," *American Political Science Review,* Vol. 58, No. 1, March 1964, pp. 23–35.

Morrow, James D., *Game Theory for Political Scientists*, Princeton, N.J.: Princeton University Press, 1995.

National Counterterrorism Center, "Hizballah," *Counterterrorism Guide*, undated; referenced June 5, 2014. As of April 27, 2015:
http://www.nctc.gov/site/groups/hizballah.html

NATO—*See* North Atlantic Treaty Organization.

Nichol, Jim, *Russia–Georgia Conflict in August 2008: Context and Implications for U.S. Interests*, Washington, D.C.: Congressional Research Service, RL34618, March 3, 2009. As of April 27, 2015:
https://www.fas.org/sgp/crs/row/RL34618.pdf

North Atlantic Treaty, April 4, 1949. As of April 27, 2015:
http://www.nato.int/cps/en/natohq/official_texts_17120.htm

North Atlantic Treaty Organization, "What Is Article 5?" undated. As of April 28, 2015:
http://www.nato.int/terrorism/five.htm

Nye, Joseph S., Jr., "Nuclear Learning and U.S.–Soviet Security Regimes," *International Organization*, Vol. 41, No. 3, Summer 1987, pp. 371–402.

Nye, Joseph S., Jr., and Sean M. Lynn-Jones, "International Security Studies: A Report of a Conference on the State of the Field," *International Security*, Vol. 12, No. 4, Spring 1988, pp. 5–27.

Obama, Barack, *National Security Strategy*, Washington, D.C.: White House, May 27, 2010. As of April 27, 2015:
http://nssarchive.us/national-security-strategy-2010/

———, *Sustaining U.S. Global Leadership: Priorities for 21st Century Defense*, Washington, D.C.: White House, January 2012. As of December 31, 2014:
http://www.defense.gov/news/Defense_Strategic_Guidance.pdf

———, *National Security Strategy*, Washington, D.C.: White House, February 2015. As of May 5, 2015:
http://nssarchive.us/wp-content/uploads/2015/02/2015.pdf

[On the complex of measures to involve Ukraine in the Eurasian integration process], [Mirror of the week], August 16, 2013. As of May 11, 2015 [in Russian]:
http://gazeta.zn.ua/internal/
o-komplekse-mer-po-vovlecheniyu-ukrainy-v-evraziyskiy-integracionnyy-process-_.html

Pape, Robert Anthony, *Bombing to Win: Airpower and Coercion in War*, Ithaca, N.Y.: Cornell University Press, 1996.

Petro, Nicolai N., "Legal Case for Russian Intervention in Georgia," *Fordham International Law Journal*, Vol. 32, No. 5, May 2009, pp. 1524–1549.

Pfanner, Toni, "Interview with Sir General Rupert Smith," *International Review of the Red Cross*, Vol. 88, No. 864, December 2006, pp. 719–727. As of May 5, 2014:
http://www.icrc.org/eng/assets/files/other/irrc_864_interview_rupert_smith.pdf

Pillar, Paul R., "The Forgotten Principles of Deterrence," *National Interest*, March 28, 2014. As of April 27, 2015:
http://nationalinterest.org/blog/paul-pillar/the-forgotten-principles-deterrence-10148

Potëmkin, V. P., ed., *Istoriia diplomati*, Moskva: Gos. sotsial'no-ekon. izd.-vo, 1941–1945.

Qiao Liang and Wang Xiangsui, *Unrestricted Warfare*, Beijing: PLA Literature and Arts Publishing House, 1999.

Rabin, Matthew, "Risk Aversion and Expected-Utility Theory: A Calibration Theorem," *Econometrica*, Vol. 68, No. 5, September 2000, pp. 1281–1292.

Rabin, Matthew, and Richard H. Thaler, "Anomalies: Risk Aversion," *Journal of Economic Perspectives*, Vol. 15, No. 1, Winter 2001, pp. 219–232.

Reagan, Ronald W., *National Security Strategy of the United States*, Washington, D.C.: White House, 1987. As of April 27, 2015:
http://nssarchive.us/national-security-strategy-1987/

Remnick, David, "Putin and the Exile," *New Yorker*, April 28, 2014. As of April 27, 2015:
http://www.newyorker.com/magazine/2014/04/28/putin-and-the-exile

Rose, Gideon, "Review: Neoclassical Realism and Theories of Foreign Policy," *World Politics*, Vol. 51, No. 1, October 1998, pp. 144–172.

Rouillard, Louis-Philippe, "The *Caroline* Case: Anticipatory Self-Defence in Contemporary International Law," *Miskolc Journal of International Law*, Vol. 1, No. 2, 2004, pp. 104–120. As of May 5, 2014:
http://www.uni-miskolc.hu/~wwwdrint/20042rouillard1.htm

Schelling, Thomas C., "An Essay on Bargaining," *American Economic Review*, Vol. 46, No. 3, June 1956, pp. 281–306.

———, "Bargaining, Communication, and Limited War," *Conflict Resolution*, Vol. 1, No. 1, March 1957, pp. 19–36.

———, *Arms and Influence*, New Haven, Conn.: Yale University Press, 1966.

Scobell, Andrew, "Slow-Intensity Conflict in the South China Sea," Philadelphia, Pa.: Foreign Policy Research Institute, August 2000. As of May 27, 2014:
http://www.fpri.org/articles/2000/08/slow-intensity-conflict-south-china-sea

Scobell, Andrew, and Scott Warren Harold, "An 'Assertive' China? Insights from Interviews," *Asian Security*, Vol. 9, No. 2, 2013, pp. 111–131.

Sestanovich, Stephen, "Is Ukraine on a Long Road to Rupture?" interview by Bernard Gwertzman, Council on Foreign Relations, April 22, 2014. As of April 27, 2015:
http://www.cfr.org/ukraine/ukraine-long-road-rupture/p32814

Sidky, H., "War, Changing Patterns of Warfare, State Collapse, and Transnational Violence in Afghanistan: 1978–2001," *Modern Asian Studies*, Vol. 41, No. 4, July 2007, pp. 849–888.

Smith, Rupert, *The Utility of Force: The Art of War in the Modern World*, New York: Knopf, 2007.

Smith, William E., "Terror Aboard Flight 847," *Time*, June 24, 2001. As of June 9, 2014:
http://content.time.com/time/magazine/article/0,9171,142099,00.html

Snidal, Duncan, "International Cooperation Among Relative Gains Maximizers," *International Studies Quarterly*, Vol. 35, No. 4, December 1991, pp. 387–402.

Snider, L. Britt, "Recollections from the Church Committee's Investigation of NSA: Unlucky SHAMROCK," *Studies in Intelligence*, Winter 1999–2000. As of January 3, 2015:
https://www.cia.gov/library/center-for-the-study-of-intelligence/csi-publications/csi-studies/studies/winter99-00/art4.html

Solonyna, Yevhen, "Russia's Plan for Ukraine: Purported Leaked Strategy Document Raises Alarm," Radio Free Europe Radio Liberty, August 20, 2013. As of April 27, 2015:
http://www.rferl.org/content/russia-ukraine-leaked-strategy-document/25081053.html

Spitzer, Kirk, "U.S. and Japanese Forces Lock and Load with One Eye on China," *Time*, September 23, 2014. As of May 11, 2015:
http://time.com/3419988/us-japan-ground-self-defense-force-joint-training-okinawa-china/

Stent, Angela, "Putin's Ukrainian Endgame and Why the West May Have a Hard Time Stopping Him," *CNN.com*, March 4, 2014. As of April 27, 2015:
http://www.cnn.com/2014/03/03/opinion/stent-putin-ukraine-russia-endgame/

Stoessinger, John George, *Why Nations Go to War*, 10th ed., Belmont, Calif.: Thomson/Wadsworth, 2008.

"Timeline: Ukraine's Political Crisis," *Aljazeera*, September 20, 2014. As of February 9, 2015:
http://www.aljazeera.com/news/europe/2014/03/timeline-ukraine-political-crisis-201431143722854652.html

Treaty of Friendship, Cooperation and Mutual Assistance Between the People's Republic of Albania, the People's Republic of Bulgaria, the Hungarian People's Republic, the German Democratic Republic, the Polish People's Republic, the Rumanian People's Republic, the Union of Soviet Socialist Republics, and the Czechoslovak Republic, May 14, 1955. As of April 27, 2015:
http://avalon.law.yale.edu/20th_century/warsaw.asp

Treaty of Mutual Cooperation and Security Between Japan and the United States of America, January 19, 1960. As of April 28, 2015:
http://www.mofa.go.jp/region/n-america/us/q&a/ref/1.html

Tucker, Patrick, "The Science of Unmasking Russian Forces in Ukraine," *Defense One*, April 16, 2014. As of April 27, 2015:
http://www.defenseone.com/technology/2014/04/science-unmasking-russian-forces-ukraine/82693/

"Ukraine Crisis: Timeline," *BBC News*, November 13, 2014. As of February 9, 2015:
http://www.bbc.com/news/world-middle-east-26248275

"U.S. Accuses Hezbollah of Aiding Iran in Iraq," *New York Times*, July 2, 2007.

U.S. Commission on CIA Activities Within the United States, *Report to the President*, Washington, D.C.: U.S. Government Printing Office, 1975. As of January 3, 2015:
http://www.fordlibrarymuseum.gov/library/document/0005/1561495.pdf

U.S. Department of Defense, *Report of the DoD Commission on Beirut International Airport Terrorist Act, October 23, 1983*, December 20, 1983. As of April 27, 2015:
https://fas.org/irp/threat/beirut-1983.pdf

Vincent, Jack E., and Edward W. Schwerin, "Ratios of Force and Escalation in a Game Situation," *Journal of Conflict Resolution*, Vol. 15, No. 4, December 1971, pp. 489–511.

Walt, Stephen M., "Rigor or Rigor Mortis? Rational Choice and Security Studies," *International Security*, Vol. 23, No. 4, Spring 1999, pp. 5–48.

Waltz, Kenneth N., "Nuclear Myths and Political Realities," *American Political Science Review*, Vol. 84, No. 3, September 1990, pp. 731–745.

Washington Treaty—*See* North Atlantic Treaty, 1949.

Wohlstetter, Albert, "The Delicate Balance of Terror," *Foreign Affairs*, Vol. 37, No. 2, January 1959.

Wong, Edward, and Jonathan Ansfield, "China, Trying to Bolster Its Claims, Plants Islands in Disputed Waters," *New York Times*, June 16, 2014.

Wright, Quincy, "The Escalation of International Conflicts," *Journal of Conflict Resolution*, Vol. 9, No. 4, December 1965, pp. 434–449.

Yacoub, Sameer N., "US Says Iran Smuggling Missiles to Iraq," *Washington Post*, September 24, 2007. As of June 5, 2014:
http://www.washingtonpost.com/wp-dyn/content/article/2007/09/23/AR2007092300213.html

Zagare, Frank C., "NATO, Rational Escalation and Flexible Response," *Journal of Peace Research*, Vol. 29, No. 4, November 1992, pp. 435–454.